One
Of
Them

Shaneel La

One Of Them

ALLEN&UNWIN
SYDNEY · MELBOURNE · AUCKLAND · LONDON

First published in 2023

Text © Shaneel Lal, 2023
Images © as credited on the page
NB some names have been changed to protect the identity of individuals

Allen & Unwin
Level 2, 10 College Hill, Freemans Bay
Auckland 1011, New Zealand
Phone: (64 9) 377 3800
Email: auckland@allenandunwin.com
Web: www.allenandunwin.co.nz

83 Alexander Street
Crows Nest NSW 2065, Australia
Phone: (61 2) 8425 0100

A catalogue record for this book is available from the National Library of New Zealand.

ISBN 978 1 99100 628 8

Cover photo by Nic Staveley
Design by Saskia Nicol
Set in Radio Grotesk
Printed and bound in Australia by Pegasus Media & Logistics

10 9 8 7 6 5 4 3

For all the queer people fighting to live another day:
never give up.

Contents

Contents

1
Chini

'CHINI!' Ma yells, chasing after my sister, Sweta, and me with a hot spoon in her hand as we run off barefoot in the muddied grass to play at Guddi and Naffi's place. Fiji's fourth coup has just ended. Things are settling but the best part is that we can play outside again. Ma's Gothel-like locks bounce and her round eyes widen with anger as she runs after us. Her long blue skirt and the judgement of the villagers if they see her running slow her down. Sweta and I have a dish lid with *chini la lali* on it.

Everyone calls me Chini. It means sugar. I am notorious for drinking lots of sugar mixed with water. My nickname turns into the phrase *'Chini pani juice'*. It means sweet water. I love sugar, and I have sneaky ways to get sugar for my drinks. Pa's Ma, Aji, makes Sweta and me *chini la lali*. She melts sugar in a pot and pours it on a pot lid and lets it harden into sugar glass. On rare occasions, Aji puts some peanut into the melted sugar. Sugar and peanuts are expensive. Ma frowns upon this kind of wasteful spending.

We call Ma's best friend Kaki, meaning Auntie. Kaki is a courtesy title. She is like family, but we have no blood relationship. That does not matter to us. We are closer than family. Kaki and Ma love tea. Kaki comes to our place in the evenings and Ma makes her *doodh la cha*, milk tea. They sit on the veranda as the sun downs, often gossiping. I sit with them trying to listen in to all the hot goss about my neighbours. Kaki says my ears feel like dough, so she makes a habit out of pulling them. She sometimes pulls my ears till they go red and I have to run from her.

Guddi and Naffi are Kaki's daughters. They live a house away from ours. Guddi, Naffi, Sweta and I compete on who can make the best dress for the dolls. I love sewing and dressing Barbie dolls. Guddi is the oldest at ten, and I am the youngest at five. Sweta is two years older at seven and Naffi is eight. When I get home from kindergarten and Sweta from primary school, we run off and yell to Ma, 'Guddi and Naffi are waiting for us. Kaki's got more scraps.'

Kaki is a tailor. She sews people's saree blouses, dresses, tops, shirts, pants and school uniforms. She does it all. She always has extra scrap material lying around. We collect the material to sew clothes for the dolls. We are most likely to get cotton. That is the most common material people use for their clothes. We'd be lucky to find some netting material.

We take the needles, cotton threads and some buttons from the Royal Dansk Danish Butter Cookies tin. I don't know where those tins came from. Did they ever have cookies? They are always filled with measuring tapes, threads and buttons. Aji is a tailor, and she has these cookie tins filled with buttons too.

Although Ma never expresses that she is happy for us to play around, I know she *is* glad that Sweta and I are close to Guddi and Naffi. She always complains as she says yes to us playing at their house. As Sweta and I run off, Ma's voice follows us. 'Be polite. Thank Kaki for the scraps. Don't get under her feet.'

Sweta giggles. 'We'll be under her house.'

Most houses are built high on planks with space underneath. Kaki's house is like this. We make a fort under their house to make clothes for our dolls. It is a magical place. We decorate our fort with any sparkly clothing scraps we can find.

Kaki's house is bigger and newer. We live in a house of wooden and tin walls painted blue with a tin roof. Our home is not very durable. It shakes during hurricanes — we have to tie it down during cyclone season, and the roof leaks if it rains too heavily. We place bowls under the leaks. The tin walls have small holes in them. I try to put my pinkie through the holes, but it does not fit. I place my thumb and the sun lights up my nail. When I have gum, I use it to close the gap. Ma does not like me doing that.

Our home is surrounded by goodness. We have mandarin, banana and *salifa* (soursop or custard apple) trees. Sweta and I spend much of our time plucking fruit from the trees. Aji does not allow the villagers to take the mandarins from our trees. She is strict about us picking them. But Sweta, Guddi, Naffi and I go into our neighbour's yard where Aji cannot see us and pick the fruits. We often get snapped at by Aji or our neighbour. When we've picked enough mandarins or are about to be caught, we run to Guddi and Naffi's house. We mix the mandarins with chillies and salt and eat it while we watch a Bollywood movie or whatever is on Nickelodeon.

The roadsides are embellished with dried coconuts. When we run to Kaki's place, we wave and yell hello to everyone we see. We know everyone from every house. We call all the elderly women Aji and all the elderly men Aja, even though they are not related to us by blood. No one pays much mind to blood and non-blood relations. They seem like frivolous distinctions. We respect all the elders equally. Our relationships are fostered on love for each other.

Our village is on the biggest island, Viti Levu, and although we are only an hour's drive from Suva, we might as well be on an outlying island. We are isolated. There is very limited public transport to the city and limited internet to connect us to the outside world. I am surrounded by a mix of Hindus, Muslims and Christians. Aji and Aja are Hindu, so the rest of my immediate family are Hindu too. Kaki was Hindu before she married into a Muslim family. Guddi and Naffi are Muslim.

One Of Them

I don't have a doll because they are girls' toys, but Guddi has lent me her old one. Guddi is bossy but resourceful. 'Do this. Those colours don't work together. That's the wrong fabric.' I let her words wash over me. She might think orange and red are awful together, but to me they speak of hibiscus flowers. Guddi sews a *sulu* for her doll. This time she has chosen red and green. All the time she keeps a watch on me, leaning over to help me thread a needle or hold my doll while I struggle to pull its head through the neck hole.

I am one of a large group of children in my village. Our village is perfect for thrilling games of hide and seek. Most houses are built on platforms so there is space under them to hide. About fifteen of us, Sweta, Guddi, Naffi, Bittu, Dolly, Polly and me being the core group, gather on Guddi and Naffi's front lawn to play hide and seek. We can hide anywhere: under people's houses, in drains, in a bush, in the broken-down car parked on the side of the road, under a small cliff or up a tree. There are no limits. It is impossible to find people, but all the running, hiding and yelling brings life to our village. The noise makes the elders angry, but we are carefree. We play for as long as we can.

As soon as Sweta and I see Pa's yellow work van turn the corner, we run home. Pa's van is easily recognisable. Pa does not like Sweta and me running around the road playing with the other children. He wants us to stay put at home. After some time, Sweta and I figure out what time Pa will come home each day and we finish the games and return home before Pa does.

Another game is *tin paani*, played in two teams with tins, pieces of square board and a ball. We collect any tin that we can find and set it up in a pyramid between the two teams. One team defends while the other attacks. The attacking team throws the ball to knock down the tins and try to scatter them. They aren't allowed to touch the tins for the rest of the game.

The job of the defending team is to set the tins back up in the pyramid without getting hit with the ball and eliminated. The attacking team targets the captain because if they can eliminate the captain then they win. The defending team is armed with boards to defend themselves but also to hit the ball far away to gain time to set up their tins again. Often, we play barefoot. One rainy day I am running around and step on a sharp stone that stabs the sole of my left foot. The water running in the drain is red as I squirm in pain. Ma puts turmeric on the cut and wraps my foot.

Tin paani causes a ruckus. We become rowdy. We run across the road and in and out of people's yards. We sometimes break people's jalousie louvres with the ball. We play from morning till night without getting tired. If not *tin paani*, we put a badminton net across the narrow road. I am such a queen. I prance around on the road and every time I hit the shuttlecock, I grunt, like I am playing in the Olympics.

If we aren't running around the village, we hold dance competitions inside Guddi and Naffi or Polly, Dolly and Bittu's house. Aji and Ma stay at home so we can't do those things at our place. Our friends' parents work and their grandparents do not live with them, so no one is at their house in the day.

Aji loves her Indian soap opera TV shows. She watches *Kumkum — Ek Pyara Sa Bandhan, Kahaani Ghar Ghar Kii, Kyunki Saas Bhi Kabhi Bahu Thi* and *Baa Bahoo Aur Baby*. Indian TV shows come on after the six o'clock news. Sweta and I enjoy watching them too. We have a thick television with a big back. It is an old-style TV, but it does the job. Pa has the original Nintendo games. We play the Super Mario Bros game and Duck Hunt. Most of all, I love the Rugby Sevens. The entire village does. When Fiji scores a try, people beat their tin walls like drums. The entire village is a synchronised orchestra.

Aja drops Sweta and me off to school in the morning before going to drive his taxi in Suva. Our day at the school always begins with cleaning. Some students sweep the floor with the coconut broom, and some pick up rubbish outside the classroom before we all wipe the louvres clean. All the students are required to bring a piece of cloth to wipe the windows. We wet the cloth and clean the window before drying it with the *Fiji Times*. The students who do not have a cloth are punished. They might lose their fifteen-minute recess break to detention, have to clean the toilets or get smacked with a duster on bunched fingers.

All the classrooms have a little rectangle of garden in front of them. The garden is surrounded by a cement wall that comes just above my ankle. Having wiped the windows clean, all the students head outside to break the soil and water the flower garden. There are earthworms all over the garden. The boys try to find the biggest one to fling on others.

Finally, the bell rings for us to head inside. We run to the tap area to wash our hands as quickly as possible before heading into class to pray. The morning prayers are done in three parts. First, we sing a hymn. Then a student reads a Bible verse and another says a prayer. The prayers are the most fun part of the mornings unless you are the one to say it.

Singing the hymn brings out the best in our school. All the classes sing at the same time in their classrooms, often different songs, but when we all sing the same song at the same time, the building transforms into a choir. 'Father Abraham' gets the school going. One student initiates the song with the words 'Father Abraham, two, three', and all the students erupt into singing:

Father Abraham had many sons
Many sons had Father Abraham

I am one of them and so are you, my friend
So let's just praise the Lord
Right arm . . .

As the song continues, the stomping begins. We are taking it to church every morning. It is magical. Outsiders hear our building come alive when we start singing. The building is erupting with joyful noise.

When the prayers end, we start classes for the day. We do the usual papers: English, maths, social science, health science, PE, Hindi, Fijian and arts and craft. I am good at school; however, my school reports always note that I am talkative. The teachers cannot get me to shut up.

We get a recess break in the morning. Lunch is just after twelve. There is a mosque across from our school. We know it is lunchtime when we hear the prayers at the mosque. The mosque has a siren speaker attached to the top of it. The kids make a mockery out of the prayers. They know when it is coming, and they prepare to join in with the prayers by yelling 'Allahu Akbar' from their classrooms. The teachers do not tell us off for it. It is normal. I don't have any Muslim students in my class, but everyone in my class finds it funny.

Lunch ends with a brushing session. We line up near the drain behind our classroom to brush our teeth. We are expected to fill our water bottles during lunchtime so we can use it to brush our teeth. Many students forget to fill their water bottle. They get detention the next day, or a hiding.

School ends with an assembly. We play around the school waiting for the school bus to pick us up. On the days the bus does not come, we walk home. It is a 45-minute walk.

I enjoy school in the beginning, but things start to change as I get older. I have just turned seven. I am in Class 2 when my friend

One Of Them

Neha brings orange nail polish to school. I am so excited. We paint our toenails during our recess break. I am wearing Crocs. I think my toenails look cool, but my class teacher is aghast.

She is so angry. She screams that boys are not supposed to paint their nails. Painting nails is only for girls. I am confused. It is just paint on nails — there is nothing girly or boy-like about it. How can something so trivial have a gender attached to it? Why is it reserved for girls only? There is nothing inherent about me that makes me dislike vibrance in my life. I cannot get my head around why boys cannot have paint on their nails — it just makes no sense. Who made these rules and why does my teacher enforce them so eagerly? And why does everyone else but me seem to know why? I have so many questions but no one to answer them.

My teacher picks up the one-metre ruler from under the blackboard, grabs my arm and whacks me across my calves twice. Ouch! That hurt a lot. I am skinny. Everything hurts more because it hits me right on the bones. I still do not understand what I am being punished for. I have not done anything wrong. I did not harm anyone by putting nail polish on my toenails. My teacher makes me stand in class till the end of the day.

I stand still at my desk, now trying to cover my painted nails by placing one toe on another so no one else will see them. It is a pointless exercise. I can feel all the eyes on my back, everyone murmuring about me. A boy seated at the back yells '*Qāuri.*'

The teacher shakes her head in agreement and asks me, 'Are you a *qāuri*, Shaneel?'

Everyone is looking at me now, some giggling. Another student adds '*Gaandu.*' I am so embarrassed; I hang my head down in shame. *Qāuri* and *gaandu* are bad words people use for boys and men who are feminine or 'act like women'.

I am beginning to discover that I am not acceptable as I am. I don't feel that I am different, that I am not a proper boy, that there is anything wrong with liking 'girly' things. Strange really, because the entire school and village seems to know that I am different — *chakka, gaandu, qāuri* are the words they use — but I have no idea. All I know is that school was a safe place for two years and now it has become an alien world where the teachers don't like me and the boys shun me until they start mocking me.

I get home that evening and my teacher has already called Pa and Ma about what happened at school. I expect they will be angry too and that I am in for a beating. At dinner Aja says, 'You are not going to Kaki's again, Shaneel. You're a boy. You don't play with dolls.'

I sit there, stunned. I cannot paint my nails, and now I cannot not play with dolls either? Why can't I sew clothes for my doll? They don't tell Sweta she cannot do these things. It isn't fair.

Aja puts both hands on the table and gives me his sternest look. 'You're growing up, Shaneel. It's time to be a boy, do boy things. You shame us if you play with girls' toys, Shaneel. You don't want to shame us, do you?'

Of course I don't, but surely . . . I turn to Ma only to see that her face is utterly sad. I can't understand. She loves me, I know she does, so why is she letting them take away the things I love?

2
'Go back to India'

I throw my book across the table in fury. It hits the boy who has been arguing with me for the last ten minutes. He picks the book up and aims it back at me. But I know he was about to do that, so I dodge just in time. He yells, 'Go back to India, you *Kaindia*.' *Kaindia* means someone from India. It is used as a put-down. The boy I am in a fight with has the canvas of a traditional *iTaukei*, a native Fijian.

I am intrigued by being told to go back to India. I do not know where India is, or how I am related to India at all. Fiji is the only home I know. I go home and ask Aji and Aja why these kids are telling me to go back to India. Aji avoids my questions at first, but I persist. I am curious and determined. There is a part of my history, my identity, that I do not know. I am growing up in oblivion, disconnected to a key part of me.

Aji gives in and tells Sweta and me the story of our Indian ancestors. She says the reason the students are telling me to go back to India is because I look like my Indian ancestors and not my *iTaukei* ancestors. Aji is pained by the story of our Indian ancestors, the Girmitiya.

Girmitiya were enslaved Indians taken by the British to work in Fiji. From the late 1800s, the British monarchy ordered the colonisers to find Indians to work in Fiji. The recruiters preyed on innocent, struggling Indians and offered them a job on a 'small island like paradise near India'. That small island like paradise was Fiji, over 11,000 kilometres away. The British promised these Indians an excellent job that would make them a lot of money to save and send back to their families.

Indians who expressed interest were locked in houses and not allowed to leave. A few days later, they were presented in front of a magistrate and told to agree to go to Fiji. If they did not, they were locked in prisons, starved and beaten, then shipped to Fiji. The British separated parents, partners, siblings and children from their families. Many never found out what happened to their families.

The British packed Girmitiya like sardines on ships and flogged anyone who complained about crowding. They gave them dog biscuits to eat. The biscuits were so hard they needed to be broken with a fist and soaked in water. Many Girmitiya died, and the British threw their bodies into the ocean.

When the Girmitiya arrived in Fiji, they worked in sugarcane fields. Girmitiya were not allowed to leave for five years. If they wanted to leave after five years, they had to pay their own fare. Except they had no money. They were up at 4 a.m. and given so much work that they could not complete it. Those who did not complete their work were fined a month's pay and jailed. Indians were flogged, kicked, punched and raped on sugarcane fields by the Crown's employees. Some Girmitiya hanged themselves because of the torture.

I feel nostalgic for a place I've never been. That is how I feel about India. I feel the emptiness of not being connected to one of my ancestral lands. The Girmitiya came to Fiji with nothing. Indo-Fijians living in Fiji have no India to return to. The world has changed. I am the descendant of displaced Indian slaves.

Aji shares that Fiji's coup tore our family apart. I was born in January 2000 to an *iTaukei* and Indo-Fijian family. I was born to *iTaukei*? This is news to me. Aja's parents were both *iTaukei* and Girmitiya. That year Fiji had an ethnic coup. A small but very vocal minority of *iTaukei* wanted Indo-Fijians banished from Fiji. That created tension between *iTaukei* and Girmitiya.

In 1999, Mahendra Chaudhry became Fiji's first Girmitiya-descendant Indo-Fijian prime minister. Chaudhry was the leader of the Labour party, which was made up of Indo-Fijians and *iTaukei*. A year later, when I was four months old, failed businessman George Speight held Chaudhry and his cabinet hostage for 56 days in a coup. George took seven armed gunmen into Parliament and threatened to shoot the Indo-Fijian members of government. The Indo-Fijian ministers were held at gunpoint and told to resign or die.

George was *iTaukei* and European. He claimed to be an indigenous supremacist. George and his followers were against the movement to give Indo-Fijians the same rights as other Fijians. They wanted Indo-Fijians to have reduced rights or, ideally, no rights at all. Most *iTaukei* were Christians and most Indo-Fijians were Hindus. The church wanted to eliminate Hinduism from Fiji and make Fiji a Christian nation.

But the coup wasn't only about ethnicity and religion. Chaudhry's Government was cancelling the previous government's lucrative privatisation deals. The people who had these private deals became supporters of overthrowing Chaudhary's government under the guise of indigenous supremacy. George had one of the biggest deals of them all.

The coup raged terror on Indo-Fijians. Indo-Fijians were already targets of racism in Fiji, but George's coup emboldened the racists to become violent. The coup was backed by the Counter Revolutionary Warfare Unit, which provided soldiers and weapons.

Men roamed the streets with guns. The roads were blocked by razor-wire barricades. The coup supporters smashed store windows, shot at cars and burned businesses.

My family tried to hide the best they could. Some villagers escaped the central parts of Fiji, where all the commotion took place, to hide in the western parts of Fiji. My family was trapped in the central part of the island. They knew they were no longer safe in the only place they could call home. The movement demanding that Indo-Fijians leave Fiji grew stronger. But leave to go where?

iTaukei who showed solidarity to Indo-Fijians were treated like Indo-Fijians. The President of Fiji, Ratu Sir Kamisese Kapaiwai Tuimacilai Uluilakeba Mara, an *iTaukei* chief, refused to scrap the constitution and endorse George's government. George took him hostage. George said, 'I have the President's daughter up there, and his son and his stepson . . . they know that I will kill them if they walk out of there, so they won't come out.'

The ethnic coup divided my family into *iTaukei* and Indians. I was torn apart. I had the canvas of an Indian, so my *iTaukei* family, mostly on my paternal grandad's side, couldn't be seen to be protecting me. I was snatched from them at only a few months old. My Indo-Fijian family received the sole responsibility to raise me. Indo-Fijians raised their children in fear after the coup. No one knew when the next coup would occur and Indo-Fijians would be wiped off Fiji.

I have inherited the facial features of my Indian ancestors and the curly hair of my Fijian line. The *iTaukei* students in my class tell me that I am not 'pure blood' because of my mixed ancestry. I learn very quickly that I will never fit in the Pacific community because I do not have the canvas of a Pacific person.

Aji and Aja have worked tirelessly in our village to build a name for our family. They've established our family in our community through years of service. The villagers respect my grandparents. Wealth is not important, if you have the respect of the villagers. Status is everything. Aja cooks at the weddings and leads the prayers at one of the community temples. Aji sings at weddings. Pa helps build houses and the wedding and funeral sheds. Connectedness and harmony are integral to the functioning of my village. If you fit the mould, you are welcome to be a part of the community. But I am different.

As I grow older, my femininity starts to hurt my family's reputation and endanger the status my grandparents have worked to build all their lives. Without their status, Aji and Aja feel like they have nothing. Having a good name in the village is much more important than your personal happiness.

A woman has a dispute with Pa. One morning, she starts yelling at my parents from the road outside our house. 'Nothing you say matters! You're raising a *chakka!*'

Her words shatter my parents' pride. They look completely helpless and defeated. It is as though someone has died. Such incidents become common for my family. My neighbour tells Ma's friend that Ma is a raising a *gaandu*. I overhear her telling Ma that the villagers told her I have to be fixed. My parents' way of fixing me is to become cold to me. No more kisses or hugs. No more playing with dolls with Guddi and Naffi. No more dancing. I am confused. Why have they stopped loving me?

I try to obey their orders, to behave differently. 'Stop talking like a girl,' they shout. 'Walk like a boy,' they command. 'Don't dance like a girl,' they growl. My relationship with Pa completely changes. If you take away the constant shaming, there is no relationship at all.

Aji and Aja's entire world revolves around their community and, naturally enough, they don't want to jeopardise the respect people have for them in the village. The years of service Aji and Aja gave to the village mean nothing if they accept me for who I am. Who I am is still unclear to me. I just know that I am not meant to be who I am, and there is a fix for me that the villagers have told my parents to unleash.

Although I do not know what it means to stop doing things 'like a girl', I am learning through punishment that being me is unacceptable.

I try to help my family by carrying myself more conservatively, and fail. I am so feminine for a boy, it verges on rebellion. There is no hiding me. I cannot change the very way in which I walk, talk, run, smile or dance. These things are woven into the core of me. To remove them, they will have to cut me open and let me bleed.

Things are drastically different at Nani's place. Nani, Ma's ma, lives in Vuci in a small wood and tin house. Her house is built on higher planks than ours. Vuci floods in the slightest of rains. When it floods, the yard is a pool of black eels. There are slippery wooden stairs leading into her house. She is a sanctuary. Pa drops Ma, Sweta and me off at her place in his work van in the morning and picks us up in the evening during some weekends and school holidays.

Nana, Ma's Pa, is bossy. Nani takes out his food and serves him while he sits at his chair in front of the TV. After Nana is done eating, he rinses his hand in his plate and hands it to Nani to wash. Nani isn't allowed to go anywhere without Nana or his permission. Nani does everything at Nana's instruction. I tell Nana to do things himself and leave Nani to rest. That makes Nana angry with me. But I don't give it much thought. Nani and Nana have a farm behind their house. They both work on their wealthy neighbour's farm.

Sweta and I love Nani. She is the most chilled adult around. We enjoy the freedom we get at her place. She bakes a flour cake and makes our favourite roti with lentil fillings on the days we visit her. Of her five grandchildren, I am her favourite. She loves the others, but there is no doubt she loves me the most.

As soon as I enter her house, I run to her spare room where she stores her sarees. I look at the sarees in awe. I dare to pick up a crisp gold-embellished wedding saree and wrap myself in it. It is so delicate, so elegant, so graceful and yet it is just a simple piece of cloth. I wrap it around my waist twice, before I make the folds, tuck the pleat in the front and throw the rest of the drape over my shoulder. Layered. Folded. Pinned. Tucked. Draped. Each step sparks forbidden joy in me and takes me further away from the vision the villagers have for me. I lift Nani's red circle tikka resting on the mirror and stick it to my forehead. All the jewels woven in the right place. 'Chan, chan' they sing for me. I am ready. I feel like Madhuri Dixit, the queen of Bollywood.

I spend hours swathing myself in the colourful lengths of fabric. Most women and girls in Fiji do not want to wear a saree every day. They are a lot to manage, especially in the hot climate. But I feel a craving for them. I can dance in them all day without worrying about the heat. I feel affirmed, comfortable and joyful in feminine clothes. These feelings come from deep within me.

Ma does not actively oppose me wearing sarees when we are at Nani's place, but she is not happy about it. She says I shouldn't. Pa is strictly against me wearing any feminine things; sarees are a big no-no, so Ma won't let me wear them in front of him. But Nani supports me by letting me play with her sarees. For everyone else I am entertainment in the saree, the butt of the joke. Nani sees that the sarees are my happiness.

Pa's siblings moved overseas when I was quite young. Aji and Aja want Pa to move to New Zealand as well. To move us over, first he has to go to New Zealand without us, find work and then apply for us to join him. When he comes home to Fiji to visit us, he brings presents for Sweta and me. He brings colouring books — Sweta gets a princess book, and I get a Spiderman book. I am annoyed, bored of the Spiderman colouring book. I am not interested in the superheroes. I want the princess colouring book, but I cannot ask Pa for one. I have to find a way to get Sweta's book. I try to trick her by saying we should try colouring each other's book. She declines my request, so I steal her princess colouring book.

Pressure about my feminine expressions starts building from my wider family. Pa does not communicate with me well. He does not talk to me about anything. He only talks to me if he has to. We never sit in the same room alone. It is too awkward. I can feel his disappointment in me. His sulky sour face sucks up the joy in my life. Men in the islands pride themselves on the quality of the sons they raise. Quality simply means masculinity. Pa is not raising a masculine son at all. For him, having a feminine son means he has failed as a man. I don't blame him. Nothing has prepared Ma and Pa, especially Pa, to raise a feminine boy, but his constant attempts to extinguish my feminine ways hurt me. Sometimes I feel like he isn't my father at all. I feel no kindness, love or warmth from him.

Our village punishes Pa for having a feminine son. His friends taunt him. The villagers insult him, and the elders humiliate him. He knows what it means to send me out into the world as a feminine boy. He has seen how feminine boys and men are treated. He does not want me to experience that. He knows he can't change the world, so he tries to change me. He does not realise that his stone-hearted treatment is hurting me more than the world can. The only emotion he expresses towards me is anger. It doesn't help that Aji and Aja question his manhood. Maybe if I am not so feminine, he will love me. Maybe if I can be the boy that he always dreamt of, he will be proud of me.

3
Chini
erased

The pressure on me and my family really begins biting when I am eight. It comes from the village elders, my teachers and, most distressingly, from my own relatives.

Aji has ten siblings. None of them live in our village. We don't see them often because travelling in Fiji is difficult and expensive. There are very limited bus services and taxis, and vans are expensive. People only travel for special occasions. One day one of Aji's sisters comes over to our place. I am surprised. It is not a special occasion. It is not Diwali, Navaratri or Holi. She has come to visit at an ordinary time of the year. Has someone died? A death is one of the only messages that is rarely delivered through the phone. After they have told the close relatives in person, they announce the death on the radio.

I am curious. I lurk in the background where I can listen without being seen. I hear Aji's sister say, '*Tum iske abhiyeh samaar lo, iske pahilye bahoot deri hoyee jaye.*' What she said was, *You need to fix him before it is too late.*

I hear that she is trying to fix me, but I am not sure what for, so I continue to eavesdrop. 'Shaneel is acting like a girl. You cannot let him go on like this. He will embarrass our family, our status and our name. What will people say? That we are raising a *chakka*? No. We cannot have that. There is only one solution. The decision is yours but know that whatever you choose to do will affect our relationship. I cannot keep coming here if you do not do anything about his problems,' Aji's sister complains.

Her words fill my chest up with guilt, and shame. I am confused. I don't see myself as a problem needing a fix. Maybe I am. I don't know, but I feel that I can no longer trust my extended family to protect me.

I am still trying to work out what she was getting at when she said that I act like a girl. She may have been referring to the complaint by my teacher about painting my nails in class. Aji's siblings want to fix me for being too feminine. If I lived in one of their villages, they would have been responsible for ridding me of my femininity.

From then on, I cannot stand Aji's siblings. Those bitter old people are after me like Tom after Jerry. They are deeply religious and intrusive. They have no business in my life and yet they want to control everything about me, from the way I talk to the way I walk. When we visit Aji's brother's place, he makes an example out of me. I am not good at reciting the religious prayers. He sits all the children down and makes them recite the prayers and then tells me to recite them. When I cannot, he tells everyone the evil spirits are preventing me from becoming a good devotee of Shiva, a Hindu god. He tells my family that the evil spirits are making me feminine. He insists that I am choosing to let the evil spirits destroy my relationship with Shiva and that if I try, I can salvage it.

Shiva is portrayed as half woman and half man. The other half of Shiva is called Adi Shakti. I have never seen someone like Shiva — both woman and man, or neither. I cannot get my head around what he represents. Shiva is known as Ardhanarishvara, a word made of three words: *ardha*, *nari* and *ishwara*. It translates to 'Lord who is half woman'. For the first time, I see someone who has the potentiality of all genders in them. Shiva is the masculine energy, and Shakti is the feminine energy, and together they create a balance of energies known as Ardhanarishvara. Shiva and Shakti are inseparable, giving us a god whose gender makes no sense in the binary of man and woman.

Shiva transcends the boundaries of gender. While Aji's brother is hammering me with the belief that boys are not supposed to be feminine, I am finding a new fascination in Shiva. Aji says the separation of Shiva and Shakti will bring the world into chaos. Aji's brother does not see the irony of his preaching against my femininity while worshipping a god whose expression is so like mine.

Lord Shiva is worshipped in the form of a *Shivling*, a black cylindrical stone that sits in the centre of a disc-shaped object and is wrapped by a snake. I make a habit of praying to the *Shivling* in our yard. I decorate it with flowers. My family and neighbours praise me for it, and I feel a sense of accomplishment. I light a *diya* (lamp) and shower the *Shivling* in milk.

Fijians are a collectivist community. The village elders look after everyone's children. The elders hit any child. That is standard discipline. The way that children are raised in Fiji would be frowned upon in white countries. More than that, it would be illegal. My parents have to be comfortable with the way the elders discipline me, my friends and the rest of the children in the village. Parents who protect their children from the violence of the elders are traitors. The collectivist nature of my village hides what the elders do to me.

One day a priest asks me to come to the temple. I reluctantly go to him. I enter through the gates, passing a large marble statue of Hanuman. Inside the yellow and red temple, some of the temple's most senior priests are waiting to meet me. I do not know what is happening. Why have they asked me to come to the temple alone to meet so many of them?

Once I am in the temple, the doors are locked. They do not tell me why I am here. They start questioning me. The first question is whether I love my family. 'Yes,' I answer, enthusiastically. They look pleased with my response. They ask more questions along the same lines. One of the priests asks me if I want to live in my village. 'Yes!' I say again. The answers are so obvious. I do not have to think about them for a moment. This interrogation feels futile. They already know I love my family and I want to be a part of this village. I love my friends. I cannot wait till I get out of here. I will run straight to join the kids playing on the road. But I am not allowed to leave just yet. The priests tell me they love me, and they are here to protect me. Okay. This is weird. Brown men never say 'I love you'. The only emotion they show is anger. What comes next frightens me.

'Shaneel, if you want to be a part of your family and live in this village, you have to change some things about your life. It won't be easy, but it will free you from the evil,' they say. I don't think I am doing anything so bad that it will have me removed from the people I love. I agree to do anything it takes to remain a part of my family and village.

'Are you attracted to boys?' they ask. My face feels hotter than Ma's cooking spoon. I refuse. They press me to tell them the truth, but I keep denying. When they cannot get me to say that I am attracted to boys, they yell, 'You are a *chakka*, Shaneel, and it needs to stop. You need to stop being a *chakka*. If you do not give up that lifestyle, there will be nothing for you here.'

They are adamant that if I don't change, my family will disown me, my community will banish me and I will burn in Hell for the rest of eternity. All I have ever known and loved is my family and community. They are my entire world. I am growing up in a little village with no internet. Little outside that village exists for me. My elders promise I will lose everything I have ever known and loved unless I change. How can I not want to change? How can I choose for my family to disown me and for my community to banish me? How can I want to burn in Hell for the rest of eternity?

I have no choice but to accept the treatment they say will fix me. I do as they say, hoping I will change and prevent the sorrowful future I am promised. I have never seen a happy person like me in my village. Happiness is the opposite of whatever I am. I believe the elders when they tell me that if I want to be happy, I need to change.

There is a living example in the village of how my life will be if I don't change. Her name is Vicky, and she is much older than me. The villagers call her a man in a dress and a wig. A *chakka*, a *gaandu*, a *qāuri*. My parents do not speak well of her. No one does. Vicky's parents accepted her, so they are shunned, are rarely invited to community events and are never allowed to lead the prayer at the temple. Their sin is accepting their *chakka* child.

I watch Vicky get abused throughout her life. I am on the bus coming home from school when we pass Vicky walking to catch a taxi. The students lean out the bus window to yell at her, spit on her and throw rubbish at her. I see that in a few years' time it could be me being abused and spat on. If I choose to be who the elders warn me against, the person I am inside, then this hatred and abuse will be my future. I will be accepting a life of abuse and violence if I do not change.

I have a choice to make. Do I want to explore my confusing feelings that come naturally to me, or do I want to be safe and accepted? It is difficult to pin down why I am so different from the rest of the children. I don't have the vocabulary to explain it. I just know that I love all the feminine things my sister was given as her right. I love the way I walk, talk, dance and inhabit the world, but all these things bring down on my head the wrath of the entire village. The wrath of God is hammered into me.

I am fearful to be me, but my feelings become nuanced when I see Vicky perform at a wedding. When I first see Vicky perform at an event my confusion increases. She is an artist, a performer and a drag queen. She dances at weddings. She is dressed in colourful, shiny clothes and jewellery. She wears a *paijop* (ankle bracelet) that rings, *chan chan,* as she walks by. And when the music plays, she spins, and no one can take their eyes off her. I am shocked to see that there are so many people like her. There is an entire community of entertainers like Vicky. Sitting at the wedding, watching her perform, I want to wear what Vicky is wearing but I don't have the courage. I cannot resist but tap my feet along to the songs as Vicky and her friends spin.

Vicky and her friends make garlands for the weddings. Weddings are incomplete without garlands. They are sourced from people like Vicky. I am bewildered. There are times when people abuse her for just walking down the street, but then there are the nights when they worship her, as though she is a goddess.

I yearn to be like her, but to embrace that would mean dishonour for Ma, Pa, Aji and Aja. It would mean a lifetime of abuse. The elders and my teachers are right in trying to kill off all signs of femininity in me. Their treatment is harsh. It is soul-destroying, but necessary if I want to live a happy life and bring honour to my family.

I am deterred from choosing a life of authenticity. What is authentic anyway if who I am is a result of evil possession? This is not me. It is the work of the Devil. Watching the way people treat Vicky, combined with the fear of losing my family and community and the terror of burning in Hell for the rest of eternity, encourages me to indulge in the elders' treatment. I don't have a name for the punishment inflicted on me. All I know is what I have been told —

You will lose your family if you don't change. You will burn in Hell.

The priests prepare enchanted bracelets by praying on them. They make me wear bracelets of red or yellow string around my wrist and sometimes my waist to make me a masculine boy. The red and yellow strings rid people of evil spirits. These can be evil spirits that are making you sick or giving you back pain or haunting you. The religious leaders believe that an evil spirit is making me feminine. By wearing these strings, I can keep the evil spirits away from me. It is the less extreme version of exorcism.

My neighbour is a Voodoo queen. Voodoo is a frightening part of my village. There are numerous stories of evil spirits roaming our village at night. There are stories of demons and spirits chasing people in the village, making people sick and traumatising them. We live in a haunted village, where even the adults fear the evil spirits. People avoid walking the streets alone at night. It is pitch black at night. The only source of light comes from houses that can afford to keep their lights on while they sleep. Electricity is expensive.

The rumours begin. My neighbour has put a spell on me, she has cursed me, and that has made me feminine. It does not help that I am an avid sleepwalker. I often get up in the middle of the night and sleepwalk through the house. Ma wakes up from all the noise I make stumbling into tables and chairs. One night I almost drop the fridge on myself by trying to pull the door open from the wrong side. Another night, I open the front door and walk out onto the road.

She is a powerful Voodoo queen, known to have used her powers to melt her daughter-in-law's mother for stealing a pair of golden earrings. We sometimes wake up with lemons and chillies in our yard. The Voodoo queen has thrown them over the fence. Aja is clear that no one is to touch any of it. He pours kerosene on the lemons and chillies and burns them.

The priests insist that if I wear the enchanted bracelets, the evil cast on me by the Voodoo queen will leave me. I do as the priests say. I want to change. When I realise I am not changing, I know what it means. I have to prepare myself for the fate the priests promised me.

4
Sexual awakening in the underwear aisle

On occasional Saturdays, Ma takes me with her to Jack's Little India, a clothing store. I pursue the boys' clothing section, rarely finding anything I like. I am bored out of my mind when one day I stumble into the men's section and into the Holy Land of packages: the men's underwear aisle. I walk into the underwear aisle in Jack's Little India and there he is, Marky Mark, flexing his brawny muscles and showing off his glistening chiselled abs on a Calvin Klein underwear poster. I know I am not meant to look, but I cannot look away. I am goggling at him, my mouth wide open in amazement. Marky's crotch is perfectly at my eye level. He is the most beautiful man I have ever seen. A beacon of raw sexuality. Beside him, there is a display of semi-naked men posing for underwear packages. Antonio Sabàto Jr, Fernando Verdasco, Kellan Lutz, Jamie Dornan, Mehcad Brooks and, of course, David Beckham in Emporio Armani. They are a gallery of bulging crotches.

The blood drains from my face. My body is going through changes. The *packages* on the men on the underwear packages hold my attention. My mind and body are drowning in libido. The enchanted bracelets come off with ease. They are now lying on the floor. The underwear aisle teleports me to Olympus. I am surrounded by Greek gods. After feasting on the buffet of marble sculptured bodies, I rearrange my erection. I feel the sensations and the urges, but I do not understand what that fascination and arousal means. I do not give it much thought. I run out before anyone notices I have been in the underwear aisle for too long. I could get in trouble if someone finds out I am in the underwear aisle stealing glances at the semi-naked men.

Pretty soon I have to return to the underwear aisle. One look is not enough for me. To most, these ads are selling underwear. For me, they hold the key to my sexuality, although I still do not understand what draws me to them. I look for any reason to go to town: getting groceries, buying new uniforms, clothes shopping, whatever I can think of. As soon we enter Jack's Little India, I abscond to the underwear aisle. The models are there waiting for me.

I walk through the underwear aisle once. Twice. Three times. And before I know it, I have made a hundred circles around the aisle. I pretend to be uninterested in the underwear models. Bored even. But I side-eye every package. When I have walked through the underwear aisle too many times, I pretend to look for something.

I take my time pretending to pick out the pair that's right for me. I look at every package, one at a time, pretending to be interested in the size, the material and the brand. In reality, I am lingering, indulging in the raw masculine sensuality. It gives me an opportunity to inspect these ripped bodies, shoulders like leather sacks full of snakes, and protuberant crotches engorged with blood.

I am up close to the anatomical architecture of these beasts. My body receives an instant boost of testosterone with every look, and my mind has more sexual thoughts. All my sexual thoughts are born in the underwear aisle. It is a crime for men to love men. It is a crime for men to have sex with men. Fiji is a traditional Christian island, but I do not care. There is a rebel in me, secretly exploring who I am.

Visiting the underwear aisle becomes a common thing. The underwear aisle is a haven for my confused mind. I can be in there and look at nearly naked men, and although I feel I should not, there have been no consequences to my actions. The staff are not interested in looking after children, Ma is too busy trying on the sarees, Pa is at work and Sweta is looking at the skinny jeans. I am left to my own devices.

Each time I return to the underwear aisle, I feel less afraid. I spend more time looking through the aisle, walking slower, giving each model the attention and lust they demand and deserve. I finger through the packages hanging on the wall, comparing the different styles of underwear: briefs, boxer briefs, midway briefs, trunks and boxers. I keep turning my head to look if Ma is still entertained by the sarees. I dart my eyes across the store to make sure no one else is coming to my aisle.

This time I think to get Ma to buy me a pair of trunks. The trunks are like boxer briefs, but shorter, leaving most of the thighs exposed. They are floozy. It is fine for masculine men to wear trunks, but there are too many questions about me to take the risk of wearing something so revealing. I should leave it and not take the risk. The butterflies are bubbling in my stomach. How can I get the trunks without Ma noticing or forbidding them? I place the package back.

Ma picks up a few sarees. I follow her to the counter. As we get closer to the counter, I realise this is my chance to throw in my trunks without her noticing. I sprint back to the underwear aisle, pick up the first package of trunks I can find and rush back to place it in the pile of clothes Ma is buying before she can pay for them. Still nervous, I act shocked that I picked out the wrong style of underwear. Ma is too busy negotiating a discount with the store manager to notice what I am saying or the trunks I have added to the pile. She pays for everything. I am euphoric after pulling my con with great success.

On the taxi ride home, my mind is racing. I still wonder if Ma noticed that I got the trunks when she paid for the items. What if she asks me questions? I cook up a story, but I am lucky she is too distracted.

As we unload the shopping, I pick up my trunks and shoot into my room. I throw the package on the bed and strip off my clothes. I destroy the packaging trying to open it. I tear the tape, rip the carton and pull out the trunks.

I slip them on and turn to the mirror. I look nothing like the hunky Marky Mark. I am a twink, but I still admire myself in the mirror. I stand in front of the mirror as the beginning of 'Greased Lightnin'' starts playing in my head. I feel sexy. I spin around, catching a glimpse of my body from every angle, admiring every small curve. I pose for longer than I'd like to admit. Before anyone can notice I'm gone, I put on my clothes and go into the kitchen to arrange the shopping.

In the coming days, I return to the underwear aisle. The underwear aisle has me lost in the seduction of the bulge. I am drawn to the underwear aisle, and I have no control over it. For so long I've wanted to understand who I am attracted to. I think I am attracted to men. The elders are trying to rid me of my attraction to men.

Should I let them continue?

5
Eh, eh, eh, eh, eh, eh, eh, eh, eh, eh, stop telephonin' me

I have a family of alcoholics. Everyone drinks more than they can handle. In the middle of 2009, while visiting New Zealand, Nana is hospitalised after suffering from two heart attacks. The cause is consuming nothing but alcohol for far too long. Ma and Pa leave for New Zealand immediately. They are told that Nana is very likely to pass away. With my Pa and Ma gone, the village priests have free rein to do whatever they want.

The strings and the praying were nothing in comparison with the things the elders start to do to me. It sounds benign to say that the elders pray over me to rid me of my attraction to men, but it is anything but benign. There are two temples in our village. They have both been safe places for me until it became clear that I no longer fit the mould of a typical boy.

The temples are on a hilltop. They are surrounded by beautiful gardens. Aji sends me to one of the temples to get flowers for our house. If I am unlucky, the elders will see me and order me inside so they can pray for me. They make me kneel while one of them reads from a Sanskrit text. They light an *arti*, a plate of fire, and wave it in circular patterns around my face as the chanting gets louder. The *arti* is symbolic of great Hindu fire rituals. The heat of the *arti* can melt my face.

After days of trying to pray, the priests know the prayers are not working. They need a change of tack. They order me to go to the second temple so they can pray my attraction out of me in a different manner.

The windows are up high so no one can see inside. The walls are made of cement. I have been sitting in the temple for over an hour and nothing has started. I am starting to feel like they have run out of prayers to say. Good for me. They may be done with me now.

The priests come in with a thick *chabuk* — a whip made of rope fastened to a wooden handle. My body shivers at the sound of the whip crack.

Is the *chabuk* for me? Surely they will not whip me with a *chabuk*. That would be inhumane. In South Indian culture whipping is a part of praying. People volunteer to be whipped in order to bring them closer to God. But whipping at the temples only ever happens to the adults across their hands.

I am filled with crippling fear at the sight of the *chabuk*. I know what is coming. The priests order me to bow down and pray to idols. It is futile to scream for help. No one is coming to save me. If they hear me, they will assume that I have done something wrong.

The floor of the temple is made of rough tiles, almost like grit. The tiles gouge my knees. Just to kneel on them is painful. Kneeling on them for about half an hour at a time is excruciating. They tell me they know it is painful kneeling on that floor for so long but the evil inside me deserves it. Debilitating pain is the only way to punish the evil spirits that have possessed me.

I am kneeling with my hands up and palms together. The priest pulls back the *chabuk* and whips me across my hands. He hits me so hard, my body slams on the ground. I faceplant on the tiles. The other priests tell me to get up. I struggle back up. The second whip sends me back to the ground. Fire shoots up my arms. This pain is nothing like anything I have ever felt before. Another whip and my hands will be cut and fall off. The *chabuk* has dug a red pattern around my hands. My arms scream for help. I wince. The pain blows my head up in terrifying blackness.

Then a whip on my back brings me back. I do not have the strength to get back up, so the priests lash my back with the *chabuk*. The pain is so intense, so consuming, I do not know where I am. My eyes fog up as the *chabuk* cuts through my skin. Agony surges through my back. I am in debilitating pain. I scream. I beg for them to stop. The whipping continues till they are tired. They will kill me if that's what it takes. They do it again. And again. And again. Sometimes I throw up from the pain. Other times I bruise. I even bleed. The *chabuk* is swapped for branches from *jamun*, mandarin and guava trees.

While I am going through one of the darkest times of my life, Justin Bieber releases the song 'Baby'. We do not have access to the internet, so the only way of listening to music is when it is played on the radio or when it comes on MTV on Sunday mornings. Sweta, Guddi, Naffi and I stay glued to the TV and the radio waiting for

'Baby' to play. We own a CD player. Sweta and I convince Aji to buy us a CD with Justin Bieber's songs. Aji and Aja are taking care of Sweta and me while Ma and Pa are away. Our little brains explode with joy when we find out that Justin Bieber has more than one song: 'One Less Lonely Girl', 'One Time', 'Eenie Meenie' and more.

We have a radio that plays music surprisingly loud. We play the Justin Bieber songs so loudly that the other end of the village can hear the music. It is sort of a competition to do that.

We start bingeing the songs in our CD player. We all think Justin Bieber is hot and have a crush on him. Naffi asks why I, as a boy, like Justin Bieber so much. She asks me why I don't like female singers. The CD we bought has some extra songs. In the songs are 'Telephone' and 'Bad Romance' by Lady Gaga. When I first play Lady Gaga's songs, I skip them because the introduction is too long. I return to them when I have listened to all the other songs, only to find myself unable to utter a single word. Holy moly, this woman is mad. I relate to her so much.

In 'Telephone', Lady Gaga rolls her hair in cans and holds it in place with clothing pegs. She is wearing nothing but tape. Iconic. I had no idea that someone could be so outrageous yet so celebrated and loved. There is possibly a world out there where I can be different, and people will celebrate me for it. Lady Gaga gives me hope that I can do something to change my life, even though I still feel that it is going to end very soon.

Naffi asks me who my favourite female singer is, and I immediately say Lady Gaga. There is disapproval about that as well. I am meant to like someone like Selena Gomez, someone bland and girly. No offence, but I have no interest in her and her music. Sure, she is pretty, but what I really want to do is tie men to the bed, much like Gaga in 'Bad Romance'. Lady Gaga shows me an alternative reality and boy, I want to make that reality mine.

I am hopelessly devoted to a scandalous future. While all the girls and boys are fawning over Justin Bieber and Selena Gomez, respectively, I want to be Lady Gaga. People think that she is a freak. That is perfect. People think that I am a freak too. The union of the freaks is necessary.

Every Saturday, we buy the *Fiji Times* with its weekly Hollywood and Bollywood magazine with pictures of celebrities and the latest gossip and song lyrics. 'Baby' by Justin Bieber is published immediately. I wait for the magazine to print the lyrics to 'Bad Romance' and 'Telephone'. I buy the newspapers every Saturday to check if it is finally the day they publish their lyrics. I wait for a very long time, and one weekend, they do. They publish the lyrics to 'Telephone' and weeks later, 'Bad Romance'. I am euphoric. Finally! I cut the lyrics out and glue them into my lyrics book, where I cut and paste song lyrics from magazines.

I feel like these lyrics were published just for me. Gaga is crazy, creative, and she defies normality. From then, all I remember singing is 'Eh, eh, eh, eh, eh, eh, eh, eh, eh, eh, stop telephonin' me, eh, eh, eh, eh, eh, eh, eh, eh, eh, I'm busy, eh, eh, eh, eh, eh, eh, eh, eh, stop telephonin' me, eh, eh, eh, eh, eh, eh, eh.' People have had enough of me and my terrible singing, but I have not had enough of 'Telephone'. They do not associate Lady Gaga with my feminine expression and attraction to men, or they would try to take her away too. They are all pleased that I like a girl for once. Little do they know I do not want to be with her, I want to be her.

My parents, Nana and Nani return to Fiji a few months later, after Nana recovers from his heart attacks. I am weaker physically from all the beatings, but mentally I am recharged and hopeful for life. I have some understanding that I am different, but that difference does not mean I am deserving of punishment.

In 'Bad Romance', Lady Gaga has black nail polish with mesh

foil glued over it. It is edgy. Clear nail polish is extremely popular. All the girls, including Sweta, own some. I am too afraid to paint my nails a vibrant colour, so I sneak into Sweta's room and steal her clear nail polish and paint my fingernails. While I am trying to dry them, I smudge the polish. I cannot bear having smudged nails, so I go back in her room to paint my nails again. Sweta catches me the second time and threatens to tell Pa about it. My heart starts racing. I am swamped in fear. I am going to die if anyone finds out that I am painting my nails, especially if the temple finds out. I cannot imagine what else they will do to me if they find out that their beatings are not changing me. Luckily, Sweta forgets and does not tell anyone before school.

Ma and Pa pick me up from school. Pa has finished work early and has access to his work van. We go to Nani's place to wait till Sweta finishes her day at high school. Nani makes Ma two cups of tea. That is unusual, but we don't pay it much mind. Nana is not the kindest to Nani. He has drained the life out of her. Nani works in the field and then cleans and cooks at home. She washes the clothes with her hands. She has become so thin. Nani has diabetes, and it has become severe. Her feet often go numb while walking. She loses her shoes and get cuts all over the bottoms of her feet without realising. Nana rarely lifts a finger. We head to pick up Sweta before going home.

The next night, Nana calls Ma and says Nani is experiencing chest ache. Pa takes my neighbour Vinal Kaka's car to take Nani to the hospital. The doctors say that Nani has had a heart attack. Pa comes home and acts like things are all right. Ma goes to see Nani in the hospital in the next few days and says she is doing fine. Sweta and I have to go to school. We do not get to go to the hospital.

A few nights later, Pa gets a call in the middle of the night from

Mama (Ma's brother). Nani has had another heart attack. Pa asks for Vinal Kaka's car again. I have a bad feeling about this. Pa thinks it is best that Sweta and I stay at home while he, Vinal Kaka, Vinal Kaka's ma, and Ma go to the hospital. I refuse. Sweta and I insist we go to the hospital with them.

As we walk to Vinal Kaka's place, Pa sprints ahead. I sense he is trying to hide something from us. I follow him closely. He whispers to Vinal Kaka's ma that 'she doesn't know'. I immediately feel that Nani has passed away. The six of us get in Vinal Kaka's small white car and drive to the hospital in Suva. When we arrive, Pa places his hand on Ma's shoulder and tells her that Nani passed away earlier that night. Ma is reduced to tears. Sweta is crying, too. I do not know how to feel. Everything is unbelievable. It has not settled yet what death really means.

The night she dies, we head to Nani and Nana's house to gather their valuable items and some clothes for Nana so he can come and stay at our place. I want to get Nani's sarees. I want to keep one in her memory, but I am not allowed to.

Nani's death ceremony is a sacred experience. Her body swells up. They dress her like a bride, in the clothes she got married in, a bright red saree, adorned with golden earrings, chains and bangles. She has flowers in her hair, and vermillion on her forehead. Everything she lost in life — her beauty, her charm, her freedom — has returned to her in death. As she lies in her coffin, I wish I could tell her how much she means to me. Nani would have understood and accepted how I feel. But she is gone now, and I will never get to tell her about the things I have learnt about myself. Maybe she always knew. I wish I had told her earlier.

It is tradition that the son lights the body of his parents when they die. Mama decides he doesn't want to give up alcohol and meat as required by Hindu religion for the time the death ceremony lasts. The priest asks me to set Nani's body on fire. I cannot do it. I cannot give fire to Nani. She is the one person who has loved me unconditionally. Nana gives the fire to Nani's body.

6
Am I a
homosexual?

Fua, Pa's sister, arrives in Fiji from New Zealand to visit us in 2011, and she comes bearing gifts. She brings me and Sweta a Justin Bieber lunchbox and a water bottle each. She's heard about our obsession with Justin Bieber. Fua does not discriminate. There are photos Fua took of me when I was younger dressed in a saree, with a tikka on my forehead and wearing lipstick. I have no memory of those experiences but the happiness in those photos is alien to me. My feminine energy is obvious in them.

I am excited to take my lunchbox and water bottle to school. I have something with Justin Bieber on it, who isn't going to love it? Well, apparently, everyone. My teachers and peers disapprove of a boy having a lunchbox and water bottle with Justin Bieber on it. The students wrangle them off me and trash them while the teachers stand by and allow it.

For a few years, school had been my escape from the temple. It isn't long before the villagers' attempts to curb the evil in me poison my school life. I travel by bus to my Christian primary school. Physical abuse is normal. Ma and Pa have given the teachers permission to hit me if I ever do anything wrong. A favourite punishment at primary school is for the teacher to order us to bunch the fingertips of one hand together and then hit them with the wood-backed duster. It is savage.

As far as I can tell the punishments have no goal. The teachers are adults who are frustrated at the failures they have become in life, and they are taking their frustrations out on us. The marks left on my body from the hidings I receive from my teachers do not concern anyone. It is normal for children to be beaten, so the abuse I receive is not something to worry about and certainly never subject to proper investigation.

I am kept away from the girls to stop me from becoming more feminine, and I am kept away from the boys to stop my femininity from spreading to them. They think that I may make the boys like me. If my femininity and attraction is not treated like an evil spirit, it is treated like a virus. The teachers and elders think that I have some hidden agenda to make all the kids like me. I don't want to make anyone like me, I just want to survive and live my life. I am a kid. I cannot convert other kids to be like me if I wanted to.

I have no friends. The loneliness accompanied by the abuse from the elders makes me wonder if it is still worth living. Pa has a cousin, Minu Fua, in Vuci, near Nani's house. Minu Fua's cat has given birth. The kittens are furry balls of joy to me. I want one, and so does Sweta. Sweta and I convince Ma to take a kitten home. I pick an orange kitten and name him Tuffy. Tuffy becomes my best friend, my rotten soldier, my world.

I want to play with all the other kids, but the elders keep me from playing with Guddi, Naffi, Bittu, Dolly and Polly. I sit in my room and hear the noise of the kids hitting the tins down in a game of *tin paani*, running on the streets, creating a ruckus, and I feel deeply nostalgic. I feel nostalgic for a time I was happy, and alive. I am broken.

I am isolated from young people, and I cannot talk to anyone about my attraction, but I can rant endlessly to Tuffy. Tuffy couldn't care less but he is the only one I can express myself to without judgement or punishment. When I am contemplating whether it is still worth living, Tuffy is a sign of the beautiful things that could happen in my life. I find a friend in that little orange furball, something the caretakers of religion don't want me to have. If part of their conversion therapy is to isolate me, it fails once Tuffy comes into my life. I am no longer alone. In many ways, Tuffy saves my life.

It isn't long before the outside world begins to infiltrate our lives. Pa buys a family laptop. Sweta is in her first year of secondary school, and I am starting Year 7. We don't have Wi-Fi at our home, so we buy a Vodafone internet stick. The recharge is six dollars. At first, we use the internet to complete our assignments. Fiji is restructuring its education system and shifting from exams to research-based assignments. We need the internet to adapt to the education system.

We stumble onto Facebook. It is an exciting time to be on it. Sweta, Guddi and Naffi are chatting to boys from overseas and some in Fiji. I am spending a lot of my time playing CityVille, a game about building a city, and CafeLand, a game about running a cafe. My parents bought the laptop strictly for us to do our assignments, so they stop paying for the internet when we start spending time doing things other than our work.

Ma gives me two dollars fifty and Sweta ten dollars spending money every week. Sometimes we get money from Aja when he drops Sweta and me off to school in the morning. As he is a taxi driver, he often has spare change in his car. If we get lucky, he gives us fifty cents in the morning. We discover the two-dollar recharge. We save our money all week, and on Friday evenings Sweta and I run to the village store to buy top-ups.

We can do whatever we want on the internet with the top-ups. Play games or use Facebook. Sweta and I take turns on the laptop.

One person gets to use the laptop for thirty minutes before it is the next person's turn. The time limit and constant surveillance by Sweta for her turn means it is difficult to find any information about people like me. But I know that this is my opportunity to find out more about who I am. If I do not do it now, I will have to wait till next week, and seven days feels like a long time.

When I finally muster the courage to google, I do not know where to begin. I start by entering 'can a boy be attracted to a boy?' And the search results spit out the words 'gay' and 'homosexual'. Hmmm, gay, homosexual — I have never heard these words before, but they seem to describe boys who are attracted to boys. They feel fitting. How do I become gay? Do I apply for a membership card, or do I seek a diagnosis?

The next natural step is to look up 'am I gay?' Google pulls up quizzes. Brilliant. All I need to do is a quiz and then I will know for sure if I am gay or not. I take the 'Am I gay?' quiz multiple times. I have fun doing it, although it is anxiety-inducing to do it on the laptop at home. The results say I am 'fabulously gay!' So, it is confirmed then, I am gay. A homosexual. That's hot. I close the tabs before it is Sweta's turn to use the laptop.

Google starts advertising the 'Am I gay?' quiz on different websites. How is it doing that? I am anxious that the quiz will be advertised while someone else is using the laptop. I try to google other irrelevant things hoping that Google will advertise them instead. But no, Google is after me with a vendetta. It wants everyone to do the 'Am I gay?' quiz. I make excuses to use the laptop for longer. I play videos so that the data will finish before Sweta can get another turn.

When Ma is at Kaki's place, I get curious and google '2 boys kissing'. No one around me is allowed to speak about gay people, and there is no education in schools about it. I can't ask my friends or teachers. I doubt they know very much anyway. All they know is that being gay is a sin. Not speaking about gay people is not making me straight or stopping me from feeling gay feelings. I have only one way of learning about myself: porn.

Puberty is changing my body. I try to sneak away with the laptop as much as I can. In search of who I am, I turn to the dark fringes of the internet. The elders think they have safeguarded children from porn, but that is not true, in my case. When I google '2 boys kissing', gay porn comes rushing at me. There is so much porn to consume. It is overwhelming.

I open as many videos as quickly as humanly possible. The website asks me, 'Are you over the age of 18?' I click yes, hoping the government does not have a way of watching me. But if you are, hey, Bainimarama. I feel I am back in the underwear aisle, but this time the men aren't semi-naked, they are completely. Everything is on display.

Ooooh, *chile*, I want to jump into my screen and onto Rocco Steele. He is old and rugged. There are categories of porn: hardcore, orgy, cruising, frat boys, vintage, mature and, to my surprise, homeless. Now hold on. Who is making porn with homeless people? The list is endless.

While watching one man pound another, I ask myself, am I a homosexual? Yeah! Yeah, I am.

7
Rebel

I find myself enthralled by the world of gay porn. It is the first time I have seen a gay couple. All the straight kids are learning about heterosexual couples in the innocent way. They see warm, loving straight couples praying at the temple and taking their children to school. I learn about gay couples by watching a man get railed by another. But the porn, the porn is good!

I feel alone when I go to supermarkets with Ma, Pa and Sweta for grocery shopping. I see straight couples, sometimes with their children, just going about their life as though this act of shopping means nothing. They are so nonchalant about being visible with their families, about buying groceries, about their relationships. Why does something so trivial invoke so much sadness in me? This will never be me. I will never hold hands with someone I like while grocery shopping for my family. My relationships will remain behind closed doors, because my feelings are forbidden, that is if I can ever find someone to be in a relationship with. Having my own family is an alien idea.

Despite the self-pity, there is a rebellion living in me. I want to fight back. There has to be a way to get what I want.

I become aware of the *Twilight* series when I start Year 7 at age twelve. I make my first gay friend this year. Jone joined our class three years ago, but I didn't know he was gay until this year, when we both become invested in the *Twilight* series. Well, I know he is gay when we fight each other for who is best suited to be partnered with Edward Cullen. It is so exciting to find someone else like me. He is a diva, and I love him for it. He always knows what to say. He reads the straight boys to filth, and I clap.

We make a pact to protect each other and stay by each other's side no matter what happens. We are both very clever. We are taught there is something lacking in us, so we make up for it by being very good at school. Jone and I become very good friends with the principal's secretary, Mere. Mere is accepting of us, and when she is around, no one thinks to bully us.

Then comes Isireli, and our duo becomes a trio. And it is an iconic trio. Three gay students in a Christian primary school in Fiji — we are the equivalent of the Plastics from *Mean Girls*, but we are cultured, and we have a reason to be mean. We are over being bullied, and we decide that we will no longer accept it. We become so powerful, the bullying ends for a transient moment. If anyone comes for one of us, the other two are there to fight. We feel invincible.

The teachers can't stand our friendship. My Year 7 teacher separates us and makes us sit in different corners of the class. They don't want our friendship to create space for our gayness to flourish. They try everything they can to break our friendship down, but we are too committed to each other's happiness to let anyone get in the way.

We decide to do our drama assignment acting as characters from the *Twilight* series. We tell our teacher that we are re-enacting a Fijian TV show *Bati ni Tanoa*. There is a little twist in our *Twilight* story. Edward Cullen is not going to marry Bella Swan. He is going to marry Jacob Black. In our class time we practise *Bati Ni Tanoa*, but we spend our recess and lunch breaks practising our *Twilight* play. We arrive early to school to have more time in private to perfect our play.

When the day of the performance arrives, we nearly back out. We are afraid of the possible consequences of our rebellion. But with each other's support, we act out our *Twilight* story. When we start our play, the students and teacher are first confused, and then they are appalled and angry. My teacher runs in between us and stops the play. We land ourselves in the principal's office.

There is a sense of pride in the hiding we get. The principal could beat us all day and he still couldn't wipe off our smiles. This is the first time we've challenged the status quo. The teachers and principal are so angry and frustrated that their plan to erase our gayness has not worked. The principal decides to call our parents about our play. Mere says she will make the calls on his behalf, and the principal leaves it to her. She does not make the calls. Phew! Those phone calls could have been the end of us. It certainly would have been the end of me. If it was not for Mere, then Jone, Isireli and I would be suspended from our school and our parents would know about our attempted revolution. Worse yet, the village elders would know.

Our jubilation does not last long. Something sinister follows our rebellion. Isireli stops coming to school. There is no way for us to contact him. Primary school students don't have phones. Isireli does not have Facebook. The only way for us to see each other is at school. Jone and I are left with nothing but questions. I am worried about his safety. I fear that Isireli's parents spoke to the principal on one of their visits to the school. We do not see Isireli for a term, a third of the year.

Isireli returns to school in the third term covered in bruises. Jone and I look at each other and dart our eyes at him. We try to get his attention by quietly calling out his name. He ignores us. We eagerly wait for our recess break so we can ask him where he has been all this time. The bell rings, *ding ding ding ding,* and Isireli dashes out of the class. Jone and I get stuck in the traffic of students. Isireli is avoiding us. That much is clear, but we need to know why. We finally get to him, and he says he does not want to speak to us. He tells us to leave him alone. He is no longer interested in our friendship.

Word of our rebellion has reached his home, and his parents are not being kind to him. With the encouragement of our school, his parents have started the process of ridding Isireli of his gayness. We sometimes don't see him for weeks. I understand why Isireli no longer wishes to be a part of our trio. He is trying to do his best to change himself. That is what I tried to do. And that means that he can no longer be friends with other gay people. But it is so unfair. Our trio is down to two. I wonder if we have made a mistake. I wonder if we shouldn't have rebelled against our school. Was greater liberation really achieved through pain in Isireli's life?

I blame myself for his suffering. It was my crazy idea to do a gay play. Had I not been so obsessed with this idea of doing something revolutionary, something liberating, Isireli would be free. Isireli is the sweetest, friendliest person I know. He cannot bear the pain of what is coming his way. It'll kill him. The pain of losing him is overbearing. Gay people are scarce. I may never make a gay friend again. Finding Jone and Isireli has brought endless joy to my life. When I lose Isireli, it hurts more than the end of a friendship. This feels like death. I mourn losing him, our friendship and our collective joy. The teachers loot our joy when we need it the most.

Jone and I make several attempts to regain Isireli's friendship, but he is too far down the prayers to return. He is a different person. He is dull, and his will to live, truant. We spend the rest of our primary school years as strangers. The teachers think they have taught us a lesson. They have not. I feel angry at what they have done. I bury that anger deep down in me. I am a volcano ready to erupt.

8
Summer
of '14

Summer is getting hotter each year. I lie shirtless on a mat under the *jamun* tree watching the parrots pollinate the flowers. The ground is covered in white and pink branched clusters of *jamun* flowers. It smells of turpentine. I lie there for hours doing nothing. I fall asleep outside with the cool breeze hitting my body and wake up to the sun turning my skin red, my body drenched in sweat. I feel parched, but I lie under the burning sun, lethargic. The heat makes me sluggish and sleepy.

When I build enough energy to get up, Sweta and I run off to fly kites with the other kids. The village elders have less control over all my moves now that I have finished primary school. I am not as obedient as I used to be, and they have less opportunity to get me alone with them in the temple. We find old newspapers and cut them into a diamond. We steal some sticks from Ma's coconut broom and use them as the frame for our kite. Then we tie threads to the broom sticks, and the kite is ready.

We live on a hill. The wind blows strong, transporting the kite higher than we can manage it. The fun comes to an end when the kite gets stuck in the overhead power lines. There are innumerable kites stuck to the utility pole and the electrical cables throughout the village. If the utility pole does not steal our kites, they elope with the winds.

Sweta and I love dancing. We play Bollywood music and dance into the night like Bollywood itself is shooting in our house. Our favourite songs come from the movie *Kabhi Kushi Kabhie Gham*. We play '*Say Shava Shava*' and shake our hips so fast, we make the speed of light break a sweat. We twist our hands in weird shapes. Our neighbours try to sneak a look, so we close the thin curtains and continue our dance inside. The heat is overbearing, but I love summer.

The summer of 2013 is bittersweet. I spend the end of the year trying to get over Isireli and coming to terms with the miserable reality that my friendship with Jone is coming to an end as well. It is the last year of primary school, and Jone and I are going to different high schools. Jone is lucky to come from a wealthy family. He is set to go to a prestigious school based in Suva. The school Jone is going to is my number one choice, but Ma and Pa cannot afford to send me there. The school fees are expensive, and it requires more than one bus to get to. They pick a public school for me.

I am hopeful for a change, or better put, for a miracle. There is little reason for my hope, but I desperately need a change. I tell myself that going to high school could mean moving into a more accepting space. We are turning fourteen, and people become understanding and mature with age.

I start high school in the summer of 2014. I am the first student from my class to arrive. I know which building my class is in but not the exact classroom, so I wait outside as others arrive. I get more and more nervous as the building fills up with more bodies. Then I hear the students whisper '*qāuri*' and suddenly my body fills up with shame and fear again. The hope I felt lying under the *jamun* tree escapes me. I feel alone and afraid, and I want to go home.

Once we're in the class a boy calls me a fairy. Ugh! High school is no different from primary school. The bullies are just older now.

I make friends with the two Indian girls who sit in front of me: Rani and Shanu.

One of my teachers is very clear that gay people are like adulterers, murderers, rapists, liars and thieves, and they need to repent. He tells us that God is all-forgiving and if we go to him and beg for forgiveness and change our life, he will forgive us. This gives me hope that I can still change. I keep trying to change despite knowing it is not working. I don't tell anyone in high school about my sexuality, but there are some students from my primary school at my high school. They gossip. They tell everyone I am gay, including that teacher. He takes it upon himself to cure me.

At first, he is calm about my sexuality. He reads me the Bible verses that say being gay is a sin, and then those that will bring me closer to God. It seems like he really cares about me. He tells me he cares about my soul, and he promises me he will rescue me from the Devil. It is an exaggeration to say I need saving from the Devil, but he needs to have his moment. I play along, pretending I am possessed.

After praying together for a few days, he tells me that we have a more grievous issue on our hands than he imagined. He needs to do something more to help me, because praying alone is not powerful enough.

He reaches for his top cupboard drawer and pulls out a silver cross. He rolls his chair in front of me and holds the cross next to my heart. My heart is punching my chest, trying to break free from my body. I am frightened of him.

He presses the cross on my forehead and prays loudly. Nothing changes. He presses the cross to my heart and rebukes the demon out of me. Nothing changes. If he presses his cross any harder into my body, it will make a permanent scar. He owns a large hardcover Bible. He picks it up and hits me with it across my head. I am stunned. The man who seemed to care about me a few days ago is now willing to physically beat me. The pounding of the Bible then visits my chest and face. I am bruised in my arms, and he only gets angrier as the days go by and I don't change.

He is convinced that there are demons in me. He doesn't just want to make me straight; he wants me to hate the idea of being gay. He wants me to hate myself, and he wants to drive that hatred so deep into me that I never return to loving myself.

He tells me to wear a rubber band and snap myself with it every time I feel attracted to boys or catch myself walking, talking, laughing, smiling, dancing, existing in a feminine way. If I do not have a rubber band, he tells me to pinch myself. He wants me to induce pain every time I have gay feelings and thoughts. I wear a rubber band around my finger and wrist to snap myself. My gayness is not aversive to me in the beginning, but after multiple pairings of snapping or pinching myself with my gay feelings and thoughts, my gayness elicits pain without me snapping or pinching myself. I associate my gayness with pain, so accepting I am gay becomes punishment itself. My teacher trains me to be at pain with myself. I am self-loathing. I am not changing but I am suppressing my identity to minimise the pain.

All the straight students around me are starting to feel warmly about other students. High school is a time for students to explore relationships, and to act on the butterflies in their stomach. I feel lonely now that the few friends I have are in relationships and spending all their time with their boyfriends. They have no time for me. They run away to their boyfriends as soon as the recess and lunch bells rings, and I am left to eat my lunch alone. Until the day I meet him.

He is leaning on one of the small bandstand-like shelters when my eyes lock with his dreamy brown eyes. The world seems to have stopped. My *sulu* blowing gently in the wind, his shirt hugging him tightly across his toned body. A packet of tomato-flavoured chow noodles in my hands, and a Coke in his. He pushes his black hair back off his face, and I feel lightning strike inside my body. I become hot and pink like fireworks have gone off on my face. The maddening sound of the bell ending the break and the rustling noise of students rushing back to class begins to distract me, permeating the tension between us. Something about him is so captivating, I can't turn away. He raises his eyebrow, shapes his lips into an inviting smile and waves at me, and I feel a warm electric tingle. He is trouble. Suddenly, the summer of 2014 is starting to look up.

I walk away smiling foolishly to myself. I need to find out who he is. I ask Rani and Shanu if they have seen him around before. Rani is cool about me being gay, so I feel comfortable asking her about boys. Sometimes I help Rani by passing her notes to boys she wants to speak to. Rani knows him. She is dating a senior student and has seen him hanging out with the senior boys. I tell Rani to find out everything she can about him. Rani speaks to him the next day and gets most things I need to know. His name is Zahid, so I know he is Muslim. He is a senior student, in the second-to-last year of high school. Importantly, he has been single for a while.

He catches my eyes again. I accept that I am going to admire him from afar. Zahid walks towards me. I jolt for an escape, trying to run away before he gets too close. I want his attention but without the pressure of having to impress him. He catches up to me. 'Hey Shaneel,' he says. Oh, dear Lord, this is not really happening, is it? I am not snapping myself. This is wrong. I should snap myself and walk away. But I don't want to.

Rani has told him everything, even that I might like him. The sun is all at once too hot and I am burning up, and yet somehow still frozen. Time stands still — so still it stops for another staring contest. 'Are you okay?' he asks.

I snap out of the nervousness, and stutter, 'Yes, and you are?' as if I did not hire Rani as a private investigator to look into him.

'Oh, you know me,' he says. 'I have been noticing you looking at me, and I thought you would like to hang out sometime?' he follows.

I scream YES! PLEASE! I WOULD LOVE TO! in my head, but I say 'Oh, you must be mistaken.' I am so silly to keep pretending I am not attracted to him. I am thirsty and the well has walked to me, and I am refusing to drink. Can I be any dumber?

'So, is that a no to hanging out?' Zahid asks.

I blurt out 'No, no, I want to hang out,' and now I am exposed. I act impulsively. This is my last chance to get closer to Zahid. A rose-red flush blooms on my cheeks. I drop my head to the ground and keep staring at the floor. I don't know what to do.

He senses my nervousness. 'I will see you at the canteen at lunch tomorrow,' he says, walking away.

I resist the urge to look back into his eyes. I keep my eyes glued to my shoes, counting to ten in my head, hoping he has walked far away. And then my eyes search for him in the crowd.

I feel warmly about Zahid, but I fear I can never express my feelings. Doing so will get me in a lot of trouble. I cannot sleep that night. I lie on the floor in my swim shorts in the summer heat. I get a rush of overwhelming excitement, kicking my feet in the air and rolling on the floor, squealing to myself. I am acting childish and silly. You could call it giddiness, but I do not care. Zahid makes me feel like dancing as if nobody is watching. I have no problem doing the things I find cringe and embarrassing for Zahid.

But the butterflies are there too. My nerves are meeting my joy. What do I call it? Nervous excitement? Intense anxiety? Unprecedented passion? I feel alive! I could take on the world. I cannot wait for tomorrow. I wake up in the morning swooning with delight. I put on my best *sulu* and school shirt. I feel like the main character as I stare out the bus window. I sit in class tapping my pen on the desk, shaking my leg, looking around. I am distracted.

As soon as the bell rings, I shoot off to the canteen. He is leaning on a post at the canteen with the senior boys. I don't know how to approach. I stand afar awkwardly pretending to look for him, hoping he will see me. When he notices me, he jogs from his post to me. Everything is a bit too public. I suggest we go to the space behind the Year 9 building. There is a large empty field behind the Year 9 building. No one goes there because it is uneventful, and often wet and muddy. People either hang around the canteen, the rugby field, the farms or the bandstand-like shelters. Zahid tries to dissolve the uneasiness, saying, 'This is a nice spot here, I don't know why I haven't visited it more often.'

'Perhaps because of the puddle you're standing over,' I respond. He giggles.

On closer inspection, he has freckles on his cheeks and his eyes crinkle more than the ordinary amount when he laughs. We find a small piece of wood to sit on. It is drizzling and gloomy, a foreshadowing of a thunderstorm. There is hardly any space on the wood. Our thighs are close enough to look as though they are one from afar. They rub against each other every time we move. My heart skips a beat. I anxiously look around to make sure no one is coming. No one is coming. Of course, no one ever comes here, and if they do, what will they see? Two boys sitting. Nothing serious can eventuate if Zahid and I are caught. I am still apprehensive.

Zahid caresses my back, before wrapping his left hand around my waist. He pulls my body closer. I take a breath as my arm digs into his chest. I allow myself to rest my head on his sinewy shoulders. He rests his head on my head. The aromatic smell of his sandalwood oil fills the air. We are sitting on a hill. We watch the cars drive by at a distance, trying to measure their size with our thumbs. For a fleeting moment, I am happy, lost in his arms.

The happiness is soon clouded by a horrible feeling. I am so close to him, but I can never be with him. I push Zahid off me at the sound of the bell. I do not mean to. My body has a knee-jerk reaction. I am startled by the bell. The students will soon head to class. Zahid tries to calm me down. 'You are okay. Nobody is here,' he repeats.

We make a habit of visiting the puddles behind the Year 9 building during lunch times.

My teacher holds an all-boys' assembly. He wants to use that assembly to remind us what real men are: masculine, numb and straight. He rewards the boys who meet his ideal of real men with pats on the back, and the boys who present as gay get slaps on the back of the head.

My teacher hates a type of haircut: the fade on the side with a shaven line from the front to the back. He hits those boys with a Bible and tells everyone else that those boys are gay. Hitting gay students or the students who the teacher claims are gay because of a haircut is no longer something that happens behind closed doors, it happens in the open in an assembly for everyone to see. He encourages the students, 'Help your brothers who've strayed from the path of godliness to the path of sin. God has given you the power to help your brothers.' It feels like my teacher is encouraging the straight boys to hit the gay students to bring us on the 'right path'. His Bible is a weapon, and the straight boys are his soldiers.

I tell Zahid that we have to make our relationship a secret.

Zahid passes for a straight boy — there are no questions about his sexuality. I do not. Zahid does not feel the need for us to go into hiding. He is braver than me. But he has not been punished for his sexuality. He does not know that my teacher has been hitting me in his quest to treat me. I do not want to tell him about it either. I feel ashamed of all the things my teacher has done to me.

I start a relationship with a girl named Monisha. She is lovely but a loudmouth. She intimidates the straight boys. We do not have to hide our relationship. The first thing we do is change our Facebook statuses to 'in a relationship'. That shocks many of my friends in high school. I am trying to show the teachers that I can change and what better way to show my progress than by dating a girl. My budding love for Zahid is hidden behind my relationship with Monisha. It is unfair to Monisha, but she knows I need the protection. She sacrifices her dating life to protect me from the anti-gay teachers and students.

Pa is in New Zealand trying to get a job that will allow him to bring us there. Sweta and I look at the planes flying above us. We tell each other, 'We will be in New Zealand at this time next year.'

It is tough on Ma to raise us in Fiji alone. Money is tight. She cannot work because she has to care for Sweta and me and the house. She starts a small chicken farm in our backyard to help us financially. It is common for thieves to try to break into people's homes at night in Fiji. People know there is no adult man in our home. Our house is an easy target. We rarely sleep properly in our last few months in Fiji. The back door is made entirely of tin. It is weak. One night we are woken by a loud *bang*! We are out of bed in a flash. We tiptoe to the back door. When we get there, the door is gone. So are all our farming equipment and chickens. We are terrified for our safety.

While I am pretending to date Monisha, I start hanging out with

Zahid and his friends more publicly. I am in a straight relationship, and I expect that to give me blanket immunity. Zahid protects me from the bullying during recess, lunch and after school. We walk together to the bus stop over an old bridge after school. People start noticing that for two people not in the same year level, we are spending a lot of time together. Every time someone asks me about Zahid, my face blossoms into a pink flower. The same does not happen when they ask me about Monisha.

Zahid and I are sitting in our usual place behind the Year 9 building. We have been performing this ritual for weeks now. I hear faint cracks. What I have feared all summer has come to life. Four senior boys run from the side of the building towards Zahid and me, and behind them is my teacher with a hose pipe. I tell Zahid he needs to run away. They may not have seen his face and might not recognise him if he gets away now, but fear creeps over him like a hungry beast, and immobilises his mind. He's held captive. Sweat drips from the corner of his eyebrow where his eyes crinkle. His face makes a soundless scream.

I take two steps back wondering if I should run. They will get me the next day, or the next week, but their anger will have calmed. But Zahid, he is not moving at all. The boys clench their fists angrily, blood boiling in their veins. They punch Zahid to the ground. I open my mouth to scream only to realise that my words have deserted me. Zahid is hardly breathing. His white shirt is covered in dirt, and a splash of blood. I can no longer hold the heartbreak. I fall on my knees and let out a cry from my chest. I push myself in between the boys and Zahid to protect him from the stomping.

A boy grabs me by my arms and drags me to the teacher. I can see a vein pop on his forehead. Every bone in my body wants to flee. He swings his hose pipe and hits me across the waist. My blood-curdling scream echoes so loud it could smash the windows on the cars passing by. The boys drag Zahid and me into the chapel where the school's teachers are waiting for us. My faux relationship with Monisha will not protect me anymore. We are forced to kneel in the rundown chapel. I see the terror in Zahid's eyes.

The teachers hit us with a hosepipe across our hands, backs and legs. The chapel has no working lights. I doubt it has any electricity or water supply either. The building has been left to rot by the school. A weak earthquake could take it down. It is dark and damp. Some sunlight fights its way in mosaics through the dirty stained glass, and there's a tiny door, which feels like miles away.

We are trapped for as long as no one realises we are gone. My teacher yells, 'You will not sin,' as the beating continues. He is a tall and strong man, and I am skinny to the bones. I cannot fight back if I want to.

Zahid collapses on the floor from the searing pain. I see him through the fog in my vision. His eyes and face look like they are burning. His groans are like reverberating thunder. What have I got him into? My heart has been ripped out of my chest and stomped on.

I threaten to scream for help. My teachers laugh. No one can hear me from the chapel. I naively say I will call the police. They laugh again. We aren't allowed to take phones to school. They know I do not have a phone. My threat is empty. They know that even if I had a phone, calling the police would have been futile. Just four years ago, it was a crime to be gay. The police were the agents of the state responsible for enforcing those laws. The laws have changed, but the attitudes towards gay people have not. The agents of the state have not either. The police would not help me. My teacher throws his phone at me and challenges me, 'Go ahead, call the police, and while they make their way here, I will beat you both to death.' I believe him.

One Of Them

There is something about being trapped in a rundown chapel hidden from the main road and the main buildings of the school that sends shivers down my spine. The fear that anything could happen to me, and no one would know. I remember the building being big enough to fit hundreds of students, but I feel suffocated inside it. I could ask them to stop but the endless cycle of abuse has taught me that there is no sympathy for people like me. The church is all loving until you are gay. It is easier to acquiesce to the violence than to beg for forgiveness or resist. Since their words have not changed me, they are using violence to beat the gayness out of me. They are failing, and it frustrates them. The frustration amps up the violence.

I know I am not changing. I have to live with the consequences of not changing. I go to a dark place thinking I am going to lose my family and community, and I am going burn in Hell. I am so desperate to change, and when it isn't happening, I try to kill myself one day. I sneak into Pa's room and steal one of his shaving razors. I sit on the bed staring at the razor. I am too scared of hurting myself, but I muster the courage to pick it up and take it to my wrist. I press the blade against my left wrist, causing a little bleeding. The pain is immeasurable. I stop immediately.

I cannot kill myself. Not like this. I have to find another, less painful way of dying. I look up and see the clothing lines attached to the ceiling of my roof. The ropes are tied securely from one end to another. I need to find another rope.

I go scavenging. I find a thick rope lying under my house. I crawl under my house to grab the rope. Now in my room, I try to tie the rope to the wood in the ceiling and make a noose for my neck. Failing at it, I become frustrated. I am surrounded by voices that are telling me I am broken and I need to change. I am getting tired of the endless cycle of abuse by the elders, by the villagers, by my peers and by my teachers. The only thing that keeps me from taking my life is the fear that Ma cannot bear losing me. I try to convince myself that everyone will be fine after I am gone, but I cannot get myself to believe that Ma will be okay. My love for Ma keeps me alive, but I feel like my life is coming to an end every time a church leader tries to pray over me.

While the violence at school escalates, a new belief is emerging in my village. The elders believe that mothers who love their sons and have a close relationship with them are making their sons gay. All the women are told that if they do not want their sons to be gay, they have to stop showing love to them. They accuse Ma of making me gay because she has a close connection to me. I have a close relationship with all the women in my life. Ma's friends love me. Now, Ma becomes cold to me. She stops showing love to me; no more kisses or hugs, or even saying she is proud of me or that she loves me. There is something broken in me. I feel that I am unlovable.

A few months into my first year of high school Pa sends the news I have been waiting for. It is time for Ma, Sweta and me to apply for our visas and move to New Zealand. We move a few months after Pa gets his visa. The process of applying for the family visa is long. I don't tell anyone at school until we are about to move. There isn't much of a reaction from the students, but the teachers, particularly those trying to cure me, are shocked. I am being taken out of their area of control. Their prayers are at their peak violence. The teachers are beating me in the name of prayer whenever they get a chance. Moving away from them is an escape. My parents are unknowingly rescuing me.

It is the hardest to tell Zahid I am leaving. I like Zahid a lot and leaving him in Fiji as I move to New Zealand is cruel. I break the news to him. He is quiet, then angry, and then sad, but he knows he needs to let me go. We know our love has no future.

It is a relief to leave Fiji. The airport makes me anxious. I think it is fear of missing something and everything going terribly wrong. I stand in the endless line fearing something may happen and I will have to stay in Fiji. I can sense the excitement all around me. I cannot relax until we are airborne.

Moving to New Zealand lifts a crushing weight off my chest. I have a new lease on life with many possibilities. I move to New Zealand a year after New Zealand passes the marriage equality bill to allow same-sex marriage. I can get married in New Zealand when I am old enough. My life has changed dramatically in one three-hour flight.

We arrive in winter. I feel a sudden icy blast of air. I am shivering and grinding my teeth. Fua and Pa pick us up from the airport and drive us to our place in Ōtara. The first night I lie in bed awake, thinking about Zahid. I miss him. I feel guilty. Why do I deserve to escape the violence in Fiji more than him? How can I move on with my life? Zahid is deserving of a safe life too.

My journey of trying to pray the gay away ended with me questioning whether it was still worth living. I am lucky I chose to stay. I am lucky I escaped it. Many do not. The cure the teachers offered me was not about praying the gay away, it was about physically and psychologically torturing me to death. Although I have moved thousands of kilometres away from my abusers, their practices and their voices are going to stay with me. They have left a mark on a very crucial part of my life.

It has made me tough. Maybe even heartless. I was abused by the very people who were meant to protect me. I don't have the ability or will to trust people. I protected myself and I kept myself alive. Throughout the abuse, I watched my friends fall to bigotry. I no longer have it in me to bear that kind of pain. I distance myself from people because I am afraid of losing them all over again.

9
FOB

I wake to a loud siren. I roll out of my bed and hurry to look at what is happening outside. It is a car driving by and they are playing loud music. A wave of foreignism hits me as I look down the street. I hear a soft *meow*, but the cat is gone before I spin around.

'Ahh', I scream. I have walked into broken glass from empty beer bottles on the sidewalk. I need to tell Sweta about them. We have to keep our shoes on whenever we go outside.

Our house is in Ōtara, opposite the Ōtara pools, in the heart of South Auckland. Before we settle in, people are telling my parents to be careful in this suburb. They warn us that someone will break into our car and house and that people will steal from us on the streets. I grew up in a ghetto. Living in an impoverished and disenfranchised community is nothing new to me or my family. In the most lucrative week of the year in Fiji, our family income was $150, and those weeks were very rare. We had to pay for school fees, uniforms and shoes, schoolbooks, bus fares, groceries, water and electricity bills, food for Tuffy and Buzzo, our dog, and plenty of other essentials. I grew up in entrenched poverty.

Living in Ōtara is a dream come true. It is so much materially better than where I grew up. The house is made of cement, there are tiles on the kitchen floor and carpet in the rest of the house, warm water in the shower and a lot of junk food in the pantry. We didn't have any of these things in Fiji. I feel no fear, but my wider family wants me to be careful. They don't realise that my family falls into the category of people they are telling me to be fearful of.

Ma grew up in rural Fiji, in Rakiraki. Nana had the mindset that there was not much value in educating girls because one day they get married into another family and the investment you made in them goes with them. Rakiraki is an impoverished farming area. Nana and Nani were farmers by profession, but it didn't make them much money. They had very limited resources, and Nana wanted to secure his future by investing in his sons. Ma had two brothers and was the middle child. She lost her older brother to heart disease quite young. Nana sent Mama to school. Ma completed primary school in Rakiraki and did well but wasn't given the opportunity to study further. She was expected to stay at home and learn the ropes of running a household for when she got married. She learnt the household chores from a very young age, while Mama was at high school. Her life was planned out for her.

Pa grew up near the city. He has four siblings: two older brothers and two younger sisters. Aja and Aji did not discriminate between the boys and girls when it came to education, although they were very traditional people. When Pa was in high school, Aja injured his eye and was unable to work for a long time, so Pa left his education and started working to support his family.

When we move to New Zealand, we have very little money. Pa's job doesn't pay well. In Fiji, Ma did not speak English, work outside home or drive. It quickly becomes very tense around home. We have rent and bills to pay, groceries to buy and school to prepare for. Ma decides that she is going to enter the workforce after spending all her life not being allowed to work. It takes her a few months to get a job because she does not have any formal qualifications or speak English well. But she is persistent and eventually finds a job. She spends time learning English and gets her driver's licence. It is a very triumphant moment in her life.

Aja picks up Ma, Sweta and me and drives us to Ōtāhuhu College. We lie that we live at Mama's place in Ōtāhuhu. The school is outside our zone. Ōtāhuhu College looks like something out of Harry Potter.

I show up in my bright blue skinny jeans and green t-shirt. I quickly learn it was not the right choice. I stand out like a sore thumb. Everyone is looking at me like I am a clown at the circus. We meet some of the senior leadership team to get enrolled in the school. I pretend that English is my first language. I don't want anything to set me back, and a mother tongue that is not English could portray me as less educated in the colonial education system.

I don't stand out because of the colour of my skin. I stand out for doing brown things, though. I speak with a cultured accent. My accent is the talk of the school. I have the FOB (fresh off the boat) accent that both white and brown students find funny. They take the mickey out of it. My accent easily makes me a target of bullying.

My first class is science with Ms Singh.

'Boring,' a student yells from the back as Ms Singh is teaching a class on mitochondria.

'We learn nothing in this class,' another student adds. That takes me by surprise. Students are not afraid of talking back to the teachers. In fact they are rude, and the teachers cannot do much in return.

The seats in our science class are ordered based on our surnames. I sit next to Maanyata Krishna, my surname being Lal. We sit at the back of column one. Maanyata is remarkably short. I couldn't rest my arms on her shoulders if we were both standing. She cannot see the board very well from the back, but Ms Singh doesn't seem to notice. Ms Singh erases things off the board before anyone can copy them. As she is rubbing the board off, I say 'Oh, Madam, we aren't done copying it.'

'What the fuck is Madam?,' a boy next to us in the back screams out. Everyone turns around and looks at me. I pull my head into my desk. I want to disappear.

The boys sitting at the back of the class make a habit of yelling out things in my accent after I speak in class. I stop speaking in class. I did not speak any English till I was six, and now because of my accent, students and teachers assume that I am dumb.

My parents speak Fiji-Hindi at home. Pa is fluent in Fiji-Hindi and Fijian. I learnt to speak Fiji-Hindi and Urdu before English. I learnt to read and write and later speak Fijian before English. I spoke three languages before I was introduced to English. Of course, I will have an accent. My accent is a sign that I know more than one language. I am more intelligent than anyone who bullies me for speaking with an accent. But I am so ashamed of speaking with an accent, I make an intentional effort to train myself out of how I speak. I give up every pronunciation that signifies my culture or ancestry.

I look Indian. The Pacific, Māori and Pākehā students call me a 'curry muncher'. That kind of racism is normalised even within communities that experience racism themselves. Many students find that kind of racism hilarious. They are never challenged for it. But they are never challenged for anything. There is such a lack of interest in making students good humans. It is racism, nonetheless.

Despite moving from Fiji, a Pacific nation, to a Pacific-dominated school in Aotearoa, I don't fit in. The young Pacific people who grew up in Aotearoa were taught that to be intelligent, you have to behave and speak like white people. They punish Pacific students like me who don't behave like white people. That internalised racism and projection of self-hatred is exasperating. I grew up in Fiji and I know that intelligence is not synonymous with whiteness.

While I am waiting outside my dance class, a boy, Tee Jay, runs into me and pushes me into a wall. I weigh less than 50 kilograms. I fly and my body slams against the wall. Everything becomes dark. My chest feels like it is stuck to my back. When I open my eyes, there are a lot of faces goggling at me. A Tongan girl, Cathrine Mafi, steps in to protect me. She picks me up from the ground and brushes off the dry leaves and dust.

Cathrine and I become friends. We are nerds. We spend a lot of our time studying, participating in extracurricular activities to build strong CVs, and doing assignments during break times in our digital technology class. We become librarians and student peace ambassadors. We do enjoy watching *The Real Housewives of Melbourne* too. Our favourites are Gina Liano and Pettifleur Berenger.

After the students are done teasing me for my accent, they tell me I act like a white person because I perform well academically. I can't win. It is dehumanising to be told that I am a plastic Indian and a plastic Fijian because I am doing well academically. That only perpetuates the stereotype that you cannot be brown and smart. The internalised racism in many of the brown students plays out in many ways. They believe the negative things they are told about brown people, and they use them as ammunition against other brown people. Our ancestors navigated the oceans using stars — heck, our ancestors were brilliant! They exemplified the epitome of skill and intelligence.

The bullying is just starting. A senior student, Adam, targets me for being feminine. I have not come out as gay to anyone in Ōtāhuhu College, but I have gay written all over me. I am overtly feminine. I walk in a modelesque way, treating every walk like a runway. I only hang out with girls, I have been excelling in my drama and dance classes, and I avoid PE. My gayness precedes me.

The bell rings for us to go to second period. I am leaving for my science class when Adam throws a punch at me. He hits me on my jaw and lip. The left side of my lip bursts open. My mouth fills up with blood. I touch my lip and feel faint at the sight of the blood on my fingers. He runs away immediately after hitting me. I go to the sick bay. I sit there waiting for the nurse to see me. The smell of the room makes me nauseous. The nurse gives me Panadol and sends me to my next class. She says there is nothing else she can do. The lip is still open on the inside and Adam is still roaming the school grounds. Does no one care that I was just violently attacked by a senior student?

I go home that day. I avoid talking, and when I do, I fold my bottom lip inwards so no one can see the blood and my burst lips. It stings when I try to eat, drink and brush the next morning. I arrive at school early to make a complaint to my dean. Before I can, I discover that Adam has complained about me to the Senior Dean. The Senior Dean accuses me of instigating the attack. I have no idea what story Adam has fed her, but he is not willing to listen to me. She has made up her mind, and I am the bad guy.

10
My closet is burning

For my first two years at Ōtāhuhu College, I pretend to be asexual. I know I am gay, but I am not confident about being gay. I do not have the counterargument to every argument that people will bring up about the sinfulness and unnaturalness of being gay. I do not want to get into any more fights. I don't want to answer questions about sexuality.

My classmates are curious about my sexuality. My friend Siteri asks me, 'Can I ask you a question?'

I know immediately what she wants to ask me. The question 'Can I ask you a question?' is always the predecessor to 'Are you gay?' I am uneasy but I pretend to be wholly oblivious to what she wants to ask me. I say 'Yes' confidently.

Siteri , hesitantly, asks, 'Are you gay? Like do you like boys?'

'No!' I reply. Siteri is not convinced. Neither am I. I brush it off and move on in haste. The less attention and time I allow people to spend on my sexuality, the better it is for me. I avoid those questions as much as I can, but I know my avoidance isn't convincing anyone.

I dread PE and health classes. PE and health are compulsory in Years 9 and 10. The classes are divided into boys and girls. All the girls are taught by a female teacher and all the boys are taught by a male teacher. God forbid boys learnt about a vagina. Maybe the sky would really collapse if we were taught about consent. We are not learning anything useful in health classes. These classes only focus on how to have heterosexual sex and avoid drugs. They teach us that there is one way to have sex and that is a penis penetrating a vagina. I am again learning about gay sex from the dark corners of the internet and setting unrealistic expectations for myself around what gays and gay sex look like.

I get a migraine from listening to the misogynistic drivel from the rugby boys, constantly bragging about how big their muscles are, how hard they worked on their legs and the number of girls they pull. Empty vessels make the most sound.

PE classes are worse. My teacher wants me to run. Swimming is coming up on the roster. I am not getting shirtless in a pool with a bunch of rugby boys. I feel insecure about my skinny body. I get out of swimming classes by forging a note from my parents. I write I cannot participate in swimming because my uncle drowned. I never learn to swim. The PE teacher does not care enough to investigate any further.

I feel uncomfortable about my attraction to boys. Or the boys in my PE class make me uncomfortable about being different. They pass comments suggesting I am attracted to them. Some of the ugliest straight boys say that I am into them. They are deluded. I am not interested in them. I pretended my uncle drowned to avoid them. But their continued efforts to establish that I am into them make things awkward. The straight boys are painting me as a pervert, a sexual deviant who is desperate to be with them. I walk into the changing room and the murmuring begins. One boy looks at another and says, 'Your boyfriend is here.' I have my back to them the entire time I am in the changing room, never acknowledging their presence, or their comments, and get out as soon as possible.

No doubt there is immense sexual tension between a few of the rugby boys and myself, but neither they nor I ever act on it. It is not possible that I am the only gay kid in my class. I try to avoid being in the same changing room as the boys as much as I can. Not only is it filled with hormonal boys, but the place is also filthy. Some boys have taken a piss on the floor and the puddles of urine reek of evil. Or of the rugby boys. I can't tell which is worse.

I struggle with my attraction to boys. The people I am attracted to treat me like I am subhuman. I am attracted to people who are the sole cause of my insecurity, fear and pain. Older men tried to pray my gay away. Boys bullied me for being too feminine. How can I like or love someone from a group of people who are the reason I am struggling to be myself? My gayness is a blessing, but the gender I am attracted to, a curse.

More of my friends ask me if I am gay. I don't feel judged by my friends. I am timorous. Maybe even ashamed. They are curious because they have never had a gay friend before. Some have never met a gay person. They want to know what it is like being gay and which boy I have a crush on. I am not ready to come out as gay, so I keep saying no. Telling anyone who I have a crush on will get me in so much trouble.

The asexual act does not last long. In 2016, I start Year 11, and we are each tasked with giving a speech as part of our English curriculum. I choose a seat at the back of my English class next to Tanya Roko, who I have just met. We are sardined into a little boxy classroom. It is difficult to have private conversations without the people in front hearing us.

Luckily for me, I enjoy writing and giving speeches. Students get very opinionated when writing their speeches. I have a conservative class. People lean more towards talking about the importance of Christianity and faith in their speeches. Jack, a Sāmoan boy sitting in front of Tanya and me, is vocal about his faith. He loves Jesus and God, and he hates sinners. God bless his soul. He takes it onto himself to condemn and punish sinners.

While we are all writing our speeches, Jack starts talking about the sin of homosexuality. He is openly against gays and preaches that gays need to repent. He does it to aggravate me, but I learnt early in life to pick my battles. I know he is looking for a reaction. I do not give it to him. He takes it up a few notches in the coming days.

One day he goes further than preaching that the gays need to repent. On this day, we don't have our English teacher in class. 'The gays will go to Hell,' Jack proclaims.

From the back of the class, my eyes shoot daggers at him. If looks could kill, he would be dead. I've had enough of this demon spawn. I challenge him. 'How do you know there is a God?' I ask him. 'Who says homosexuality is a sin?'

Jack is infuriated. No one has ever dared to disagree with his extremist religious beliefs, and then one day a gay rocks up and questions if the God he loves so dearly is real. For the first time, someone has questioned his lifestyle and he isn't prepared to accept it. Anger curls hot in his face like a blazing inferno.

Jack, with a stern look, growls, 'You do not know anything about God. You need to shut up.'

'And what if I do not?' I retort. Everyone is watching now, and Jack cannot lose an argument to a gay kid in front of everyone. That would make him look weak.

'I said keep my religion out of your mouth.' Jack balls his fingers and rushes aggressively towards Tanya and me.

When he arrives at my table, veins are crawling up his arms, neck, face and forehead like snakes. He thumps his fist on my table. I am seated in my chair with a smirk on my face. It irritates Jack. I know it does, so I twist my lips even more.

'God is the truth, and people like you ruin his plan!' Jack is screaming now. Nostrils flaring, Jack reaches for my collar, but Christina, who sits beside him, pulls him away. She tries to calm him down, but Jack is too far down his onslaught to stop now. His friends are watching. He has to prove himself to them.

The argument escalates. 'Your God cannot and will not tell me how to live my life. I am doing nothing wrong. I am hurting no one. If your God cannot let me live my life the way I want, then your God has a problem and not me,' I tell him. I am on my feet.

I am shaking, my voice is unsteady, and someone has turned the temperature up in my face. I have never defended myself and the gays like this before. I am getting angry, too, but mostly scared. I know the boys in my English class have a propensity for violence. They are all in the school rugby teams. They are closer than brothers. They are going to support each other in this situation. Tanya and I are circled by school rugby players. I still cannot get myself to back down. I am filled with passion and rage. Tanya is equally frustrated and angry. We are yelling — something I have never done in high school before. I am a transformed person in this moment.

Jack snaps. He picks up a chair and aims it at Tanya and me. That is it. I've had enough of the hatred. The one thing I feared would happen to me if I came out as gay is happening while I am still in the closet. This boy is abusing me for my sexuality. I am sick and tired of it. It doesn't matter what I say about myself. My classmates see a raging homosexual in front of them.

Christina pulls Jack out of the class before anyone is injured. The class becomes silent. Tanya and I get looks from everyone for the rest of the class as if we have done something wrong. Other than Christina, no one tried to stop Jack's violence. He is a boy and because he is a boy, he owns the right to be angry and violent. I am afraid for myself. After class I tell Siteri about what happened. I question if I should carry a weapon to protect myself. I am worried that Jack will get violent again. I don't make a complaint about him. Why would I? The teachers do not care. I was bullied in Years 9 and 10, and the school counselling service and deans didn't do anything. Complaining about Jack will only make him and his boys angrier. If I have a weapon, I can protect myself if he has another holy meltdown in class. Siteri convinces me not to and offers to come to my English classes with me, but the teachers don't allow that.

After the altercation with Jack, the word on my sexuality spreads like wildfire. Everyone knows I am gay. Let the news burn it all. There is no longer a need to come out. My anger has burnt down the walls of my closet and exposed me to the world.

Word from school does not make it to my parents.

Although at home my gayness is still unspoken, once the truth is out at school and after letting out my anger, I feel better about myself. I don't have much explaining left to do. I am getting older and more confident about myself.

My friends start getting into relationships. They blush when they see their boyfriends, share looks across the room and run away behind M Block during the breaks. It is an exciting time for them. I can tell because some of them never stop talking about their boyfriends.

There are no other openly gay students in school. I want what my straight friends have and when I cannot have it, I start feeling lonely.

11
Not today, Satan

In Year 12, I sign up to more extra-curricular activities than I can handle; I am a librarian, a writer for a student magazine, a student peace ambassador, managing the badminton team and in the school debating team. I am doing everything I can to show people I am a well-rounded student. My school sweater is decorated with badges that pull the sweater down on the left side.

This second-last year of high school is one of the most important years for students. We use our grades from Year 12 to apply for university. Extra-curricular activities look good on the CV when we apply for scholarships. I sign up to volunteer at Middlemore Hospital after school. Another student and I work the reception. The most common thing we have to do is tell people where in the hospital their family or friends are admitted. Students from King's College are also volunteering at the hospital. They show up late, do not want to wear the communal volunteer vests, choose the easiest tasks and leave much earlier than us. These students are wealthy spoilt brats, possibly mad that they have been sent to Middlemore Hospital instead of Africa for community work.

In the summer of 2017, while I am working at Middlemore Hospital's reception, a church leader walks up to me and offers to pray. I do not believe in a Christian God, and I do not understand why he wants to pray for me. 'What do you want to pray for?' I question him.

He says, 'Being gay is a sin. It is not what God chose for you. You are on the wrong path. I can help you get back on the right path if you just let me pray for you today.'

I refuse. My head is threatening to explode. Not today, Satan. Not today.

He looks at me and says, 'It's hot, but do you know what's hotter? Hell!'

At six, the idea of going to Hell was frightening, but at seventeen, Hell makes sense with my fantasy. If all the gays are going to Hell, then that's where I want to be. It is going to be a ball. I thought I'd escaped the religious extremists when I moved to New Zealand. His attempt to pray my gay away strikes terror in me for a moment. I remember everything that happened to me in Fiji. I am not over it. All the pain is buried deep in me, and this church leader brings it back to the surface.

I am more than 2,000 kilometres away from Fiji, but I can still hear the words of the priests telling me I will go to Hell for the life I am living, and I can still feel their whips against my skin. Despite my efforts to forget, they are still controlling everything I do. The hurt child in me controls my life. I am deeply traumatised, and instead of acknowledging that pain and suffering, I pretend that I am okay. There is so much shame in acknowledging I am a victim of abuse. I am not healed.

I am in disbelief that a person can walk up to me in a place of medical practice and offer me a pseudoscientific treatment. I cannot believe that in 2017 it is legal to offer people a cure to their gayness in New Zealand. I rush home that evening and search the laws around praying the gay away. The words 'conversion therapy' come up as a related search. I investigate it and realise what happened to me was not an isolated practice happening only in Fiji. It is a global pandemic. There are thousands of people who have been through these practices under the name of conversion therapy.

I cannot find any laws prohibiting conversion therapy in New Zealand. I look for conversion therapy services and easily find a number of people who are willing to 'help' me.

I want to change the law, but I don't know how to. I have no connections to the gay community and no influence on New Zealand politics. I feel powerless, but the fire inside me is anything but insignificant. I am hungry for change.

Politics is far removed from my reality as a student at a poor school in South Auckland. It is inaccessible. The school leadership team sends out letters to potential prefects for Year 13. I don't get a letter. I am frustrated. I have done everything to set myself up to become a prefect.

I have maintained a high attendance; I have participated in multiple extracurricular activities, which lifted the school's reputation; and I am their highest achieving student academically. I do not understand why I am not chosen to be a prefect. I march to the principal's office to ask him why I have been left out, to which he answers that I am too extroverted. I am too much. He says if I became a prefect, it would take away attention from the other prefects. Why are people becoming prefects for attention?

The principal does not stop to think that perhaps the reason I am so flamboyant is that I have spent years hiding my true self. My non-queer counterparts didn't have to hide. I fought hard to come to terms with my gayness. Now that I finally accept myself, I express all the years of suppressed gayness. Why am I being punished for beginning to explore my identity?

One Of Them

My school takes a group of students who performed well at NCEA Level 1 to a scholars' camp. I stay up all night the night before we leave. This is my first ever school camp. We did not have camps in primary school in Fiji and I did not spend long enough at high school in Fiji to find out. I do not know what to pack.

There are two vans for about 24 people. The vans are old enough to be antiques.

We jam ourselves into the vans and arrive at the campsite near Mount Tongariro after dark. Oh, it is electrifying to arrive in the woods after dark. We find our way to our cabins and are made to hand in our phones first thing. The whole arrangement gives me an uncanny feeling. That's why I like it. It scares me.

There are a few other schools present at the camp. We sit around the bonfire on the first night. The other schools do not engage with us. It does not bother us. There are plenty of us to have fun on our own. We ask our teacher to play music from their phone on the Bluetooth speaker, and we have a boogie. I enjoy the company of these students. I did not know many of them before this camp, but camp brings us closer, and I feel like I have allies in them.

Waking up the next morning is tough. It is winter and I have to get up early to make lunch for my group. We are off hiking on the first day of camp. The taps do not mix the hot and cold water. It is either freezing water or water hot enough to burn you. Amanda and I are making lunch on the first day, but our whole group is on dinner duty that night. Each school is on dinner duty on different nights of the week. We have to cook, serve and clean up. We rush to the shower when we arrive back covered in mud from fighting through bushes and knee-deep mud puddles.

Our dinner is not anything fancy. Mashed potatoes, beans and sausages. We serve all the tables. Siteri and some of the other girls sing a song and say a prayer before eating. The white kids find this odd. They look at each other confused when the singing begins, but we do it anyway. I have a friend at the camp with me who is feminine just like me, and we are having a fantastic time.

Then, 'We would rather eat a can of shit than eat what those faggots made,' says one of the boys from another school. We are hours away from home at a camp in the middle of the woods. One spit of the word *faggot* and our whole trip is ruined.

I want to run away and hide in the bush, and never come back. The feeling of shame is overbearing, and the fear of harm debilitating. We are afraid to engage in any more activities because we cannot tell if we would be safe. We tell the teachers about the comments on the last day of the camp. Ms Jones-White is shocked. She tells the camp supervisors, but there are no consequences for the rich white boys because 'boys will be boys'.

I am alone, fed up, but the rebel in me is still very much alive. I search for a way to influence the law. Later that year, I discover that the Minister of Education, Chris Hipkins, has sponsored a Youth Advisory Group. I apply and am accepted. This is my entry into the world of politics, my chance to make a difference. I learn the terminology LGBTQIA+: Lesbian, Gay, Bisexual, Trans, Queer, Intersex and Asexual. I immediately do not vibe with the initialism, but I like 'queer'. Gay feels too restrictive, and trans feels too humiliating. Queer is an ambiguous term that says I am not straight but implies I am more than gay. It allows me to identify with how I am feeling inside without telling the outside world exactly what that feeling is.

My position on the Minister's advisory group gives me direct connections to the decision-makers. I start advocating for queer students. In 2017 my friend Tanya applies to Victoria University of Wellington. She is only allowed to choose between man and woman for her gender identity. In a meeting with the Secretary for Education, Iona Holsted, I share with her that this needs to change.

One Of Them

A few months after our meeting I receive a letter from Iona stating that the Ministry of Education has recognised the problem and students at Victoria University of Wellington will be able to choose 'gender diverse' as their gender identity. Many people will find this a minuscule change, but it is a significant moment for me. I am taking control of my life and demanding better. The elders — all of whom are now dead — dictated every aspect of my life in Fiji, so to have the smallest amount of autonomy and influence is empowering. I am no longer controlled by those who tried to hurt me.

12
The search for my people

Everyone knows I am gay. There is no hiding anymore. Scrolling through Facebook in early 2018, I stumble on an advertisement for the 'Big Gay Out'. I have never been to a queer event before. The Big Gay Out sounds like heaven. I immediately sign myself and my friends up to volunteer for Ending HIV, at the Big Gay Out and the Pride parade. The Big Gay Out is cancelled due to heavy rain. Bummer. But the Pride parade is still on.

My parents don't know I am going to the Pride parade. I don't ask for their permission. I doubt they will allow me to go to the parade if I ask them. I have a youth conference to attend during the day. Ma and Pa are rarely aware of the things I get up to.

I have not, to this day, sat my parents down and told them about my gayness. The concept of coming out is very confusing to me. I understand my gayness as something that is a part of me. No matter how hard people tried to change it, they couldn't. It comes to me as naturally as the colour of my skin. I never came out as brown. I never sat Ma and Pa down and come out as brown. Imagine this:

I sit Ma and Pa down and say, 'I hope you still love me, but I am brown,' and Ma yells, 'Anything but brown. Give him a heart attack. Anything but brown.'

Sweta did not sit Ma and Pa down and come out as straight. It was assumed that she would be heterosexual. Almost like people are straight until they say otherwise.

I doubt myself, though. Am I not telling my parents about my gayness because of this theory I have cooked up in my head, or is it because I fear that my parents will reject me when I come out to them? Coming out means running the risk that they may not accept me. I fear they may even throw me out of home. There is so much to lose. The fear of losing so much overwhelms me and overpowers my will to tell them. It is a gut-wrenching feeling.

I use these theoretical arguments as a shield to protect myself from facing the painful reality that they may disown me. I protect myself from the humiliation. I convince others that I am not affected by the miserable things that are happening to me. The truth is that I was deeply traumatised by the things that happened to me. I feel a lot of shame in being the victim. If I come out, I fear I will be the victim again. I don't want to make myself vulnerable to more harm. I understand my parents are a product of colonial conditioning. I understand they cannot change overnight, but I fail to afford them the opportunity to undo that colonial conditioning. I feel weak, and maybe I am weak.

I have rarely been outside South Auckland on my own. I take Cathrine to the Pride parade on Ponsonby Road. She grew up in a Christian family who taught her that being queer was wrong. But She has come around to accepting who I am, and our friendship has blossomed. Soon my friends Ammon, Tanya, Amanda and Lucy join us. We arrive at the New Zealand AIDS Foundation office in St Marys Bay. It is nigh on impossible to find other brown people in this area; I wonder if there will be many queer people who look like me at the parade. I get dressed up for the parade. I put some blue and pink paint on my face, stick an Ending HIV tattoo on my left arm and pick up a massive condom balloon. It blows my mind to be around so many confident and flamboyant queer people.

As I walk down Ponsonby Road with the Ending HIV float, I feel the fear of being caught and the joy of liberation. After a while I become carefree. I am euphoric in the company of so much queer excellence. Everything is vibrant. There is music, shirtless men and drag queens. I am chucking out condoms to the bystanders as I am dancing down Ponsonby Road. Lilly Loudmouth is singing 'Raining Men', and I am living, jumping, kicking, dancing. I have no care for what anyone thinks.

This parade is not one of those things I grew up wanting to go to. I didn't know that a world like this existed until this very moment. It feels like a dream. I do not want the night to end. I have been longing for a community for so long and finally I have found something, even though it is not the perfect fit for me. I am a nobody in this parade. No one knows who I am. They have never seen me before, and I have never seen them, and with that at the back of my mind, I party harder than I ever have.

I don't want to go home after that, but I get in the train and wave the night a gloomy goodbye. The parade is over and so is the excitement and joy that came with it. Ma and Pa know by now that I have snuck out and they are coming to pick me up from the train station. I panic. My head is about to split in two. I scratch the paint off my face and try to remove the tattoo. I brush out as much glitter as I can from my hair. I hide everything that could give my parents a clue as to where I have been.

Being part of the Pride parade makes my loneliness worse. I go from being surrounded by my community to sitting alone in my dark room. I stay up all night googling to find the next queer event. I go on Instagram and look up the tags #Prideparade and #BigGayOut to find queer people who went to these events. The next morning is depressing, and my loneliness doesn't get better as the days go by. I constantly feel like I am missing out on something. But this is my last year at high school and people are telling me life changes once you start university. The closer it gets to the end of the year, the more hopeful I become about my prospects of finding a community.

I feel a sense of cultural homelessness in the queer community. There is nothing in these LGBTQIA+ identities that makes me connect to my Fijian and Indian heritage. I don't feel at home with these labels. I need something that recognises that I am not only queer, but also an indigenous Fijian and Indian. The gay community is white. Every time I google the word 'gay', only white men show up. All default gay porn is made of white men too. The Pride parade is led and dominated by white queer people.

I cannot see myself as a part of the queer community. I am trying to force my identity into the white LGBTQIA+ framework of queerness but doing that is violently stripping me of my culture and breaking down my relationship with my queer ancestors even further. The more I try to fit into the LGBTQIA+ framework of queerness, the weaker my connection with my ancestors becomes. I feel as though I am being let go by my protectors, and this is frightening for me. For indigenous people, there are repercussions for not knowing who you are and who you come from, and my punishment is being in a constant state of spiritual homelessness. How can I feel so alone while in the presence of such colourful and lively queer people? I feel solidarity with some of the white queer folk, but I can never understand why these queer people are so different from me, as if we are not one people. There is innate sadness and pain with trying to fit in with white queer people.

I start googling about my identity. When I put into 'Indian queer community' Google up comes pictures of the most beautiful *hijra* and *chakka* community. I immediately connect to them. This is who I am. These are my people, and I am one of them. I feel euphoric joy. I know that if a queer identity specific to Indians exists, there has to be one for Fijians. I smash the buttons on my keyboard. This is how I find out that I am *vakasalewalewa*.

Vakasalewalewa are transwomen, nonbinary folk and gender-diverse folk native to Fiji. This also captures gay men. The word *vakasalewalewa* means 'to live in the fashion of a woman', implying that most *vakasalewalewa* are feminine rather than strictly women. That is not to say that *vakasalewalewa* cannot be women; they can, but the term itself captures all diverse identities. *Hijra* or *chakka* are indigenous to India. The words *aravani*, *aruvani*, *jogappa* and *kinnar* have also been used to describe the indigenous queer community of India.

Before colonisation and Christianity spread like a disease through the world, indigenous queer people existed amongst indigenous communities without being othered.

Colonialism uprooted indigenous queer identities through criminalisation and punishment. It attempted to erase both *vakasalewalewa* and *hijra*. Neo-colonialism is imposing white queer identities onto indigenous peoples. The white queer identities often captured by the LGBTQIA+ acronym leave no room for indigenous queerness. My people are *vakasalewalewa* and *hijra*. There is no V or H in LGBTQIA+. Indigenous identities are rendered invisible by the + that follows the acronym of colonial queer identities. They are shoe-horned into an acronym that privileges colonial queer identities, primarily cisgender gay men.

I reconceptualise my queer identity for myself. Indigenous

queerness is precolonial and distinct from colonial, white or Western queerness. It is not the words that I can't translate. An attempt to translate indigenous queer identities to colonial queerness would cause our identities to lose our culture, value and significance. Indigenous queerness didn't emerge when the coloniser set foot onto our land. Our existence didn't begin at colonisation, so why does our identity?

That night in my bedroom, I feel like this is one of my most triumphant moments. But it also feels like one of my most painful moments. I don't have an understanding of all the political implications of my identity, but I have finally learnt who I am, and I can finally give words to the years of feeling. These two words capture how I have felt throughout so much of my life. I have no one to share it with. I want to share it with someone, but I can't. I can't tell Sweta, or Ma and Pa or Aji and Aja. I am on top of the world, but I am lonely. It is excruciating. I pat myself on my back and tell myself, 'You go champ. This is just the beginning to all the beautiful things you will discover in life.'

13

Hopeless romantic

I am becoming a new person, and as exciting as that experience is, the fear and anxiety of being caught in the act of becoming me is debilitating. I sign up to as many extracurricular programmes as I can. Being occupied all the time keeps me distracted from the loneliness and emptiness. I bottle up my feelings. Sometimes emotions burst out of me, and I am left breathless from all the crying.

I can't find love in school, so I venture onto the dating apps. I get Tinder first. After endless swiping and having no luck, I download Grindr. Grindr is a hook-up app, not a dating app. Finding love on Grindr is like throwing bread in a river and expecting toast. The app is flooded with nameless, faceless profiles. It is common for people to send unsolicited nudes and demand sex from others. I am often approached by older men for sex. Some approach me on Grindr and offer rewards for sex. I never act on any of the offers because I am too afraid and inexperienced. When I reject men, they get offended and insult me.

One night when I am looking through the profiles on Grindr, I come across an account that reads 'No fats, no fems, no Asians.' And then another. Suddenly, I realise that this is a common theme across most Grindr profiles. I haven't entered the queer community and I already feel like I am not a part of it. The queer community has a 'No Asians' policy. The racism is evident and normal, and I am at the receiving end of it. I become hesitant to engage with other queer people. I can never tell who would have internalised the 'No Asians' policy.

I start exploring dating as a serious option after turning eighteen. I download Tinder again and am met with shallowness. I cannot find anyone that I like. I give up almost immediately and turn to Grindr again. This is a mistake. I get a lot of attention from old men. My photos scream 'twink in his prime', and that attracts men with a daddy complex.

Lying hopelessly on the school's front lawn, I receive a message from a guy named Frederic on Instagram. I have my Instagram handle in my Tinder bio. I think that is how he's found me. Frederic asks me if I will hang out with him, and I say yes. Getting ready to meet Frederic reminds me of the night I was getting ready for my hangout with Zahid. So much has changed in the last few years, but I felt the same butterflies in my stomach the night before I first met Zahid. Some things never change. I have no idea what Zahid is up to now. I am nostalgic about what I experienced with him. I don't know if it was love, but it sure was something special.

I meet Frederic in a cafe on Karangahape Road. I spot the back of his head in a chair. He has a beautiful head. I can recognise him from a distance. He is neatly dressed in a blue polo t-shirt and brown high-waisted pants. My heart skips a beat as I walk closer. He gets up to hug me. I am high on his woody scent.

His long eyelashes curve towards the sky, and his luscious blonde locks drape his face. He has spellbinding sky-blue pools in his eyes paired with a wide smile and deep dimples. He is beautiful, yes. But he is different. The mutual chemistry is instant.

He asks me what I want for breakfast. I only have peppermint tea. I love eating, but I do not want to eat in front of him. Silly me. He has eggs and sausages. I am a stickler for efficiency, grammar, manners, but I do not seem to care about any of those things with him. He eats slowly, talks with his mouth full and burps when he is done. I do not mind. I like him for his quirks.

I don't know what to do, especially with a man so intimidatingly beautiful. We walk into Paper Bag Princess on Karangahape Road. I am fingering through the shirts when he grabs my left hand behind the rack, and we form a fist with our palms. He seems afraid. I give him a smile. I want to kiss him, but I'd better not in public. I am not a very good kisser.

Dating is really daunting, but I am determined to give it a go. I am more at ease when Frederic tells me he is not out to his family. I don't know if it is selfish and rude, but I find comfort in his struggle. It makes him less frightening and more like me, vulnerable and afraid. His family is from England but living in Australia while he is working in New Zealand. It gives him freedom to be gay.

I am excited about Frederic. I can't stop thinking about him. I don't know what to do. I start seeing him more often. He makes me happy and a little nervous sometimes. My heart races ever so slightly even after we have spoken for a while. He is so quiet about his feelings, it bothers me. Frederic is a very energetic and lively person otherwise. It is hard for me to keep up with his life and interests. Frederic and I are quite different as people.

He is private. Annoyingly private, and he rarely shares the things that bother him. I know he worries a lot and feels bad about many things. He isn't an empath, but he isn't far from it either. I think feeling all of the world's sorrows so personally makes him sad. I try very hard to get to know his heart, but he is not ready to let me in. It frustrates and angers me.

We start drifting apart. Neither of us is out to our families and neither of us intend, to be out anytime soon. Our relationship is behind closed doors, and on Karangahape Road, where our families would never go. We don't know how a hidden relationship like ours could work. My first heartbreak hurts like someone has impaled my chest with a chainsaw and then run me over with a truck. I still adore him, though. I am hopelessly devoted to him.

14
Kings vs Commoners

It's 11 May 2018. I am eating pies in a meeting in Minister Chris Hipkins' office in the Beehive in Wellington when another member of the Youth Advisory Group, Liam McLeavey, shows me a notification on his phone. A South Auckland school has gone into a lockdown. Liam is dressed in über-formal attire and I am in my track pants. He has a business mindset. We are the unlikeliest of friends, but our friendship has blossomed into endless banter and roasting.

I text my friends and find out it is Ōtāhuhu College that has gone into lockdown, but the media is telling a different story. The *New Zealand Herald* published an article at 10 a.m. titled 'Armed police swarm after "issue in the vicinity" of King's College in Auckland', and just eleven minutes later, *Stuff* followed with an article headlined 'Armed Offenders Squad at Auckland's King's College'. The headline includes a picture of King's College. Ōtāhuhu College was what was 'in the vicinity of King's College'.

I am troubled by the news. I sit opposite the Minister shaking my leg under the table and spinning my phone in my hand. I cannot focus on a single thing the Minister is saying. My mind is at my school and my heart with my friends. I am worried for their safety. When it becomes unbearable, I excuse myself from the room. I walk back and forth in the foyer, my breath becoming shorter and quicker.

A car that failed to stop for the police earlier in the day was spotted outside Ōtāhuhu College and three men from the car entered the college. Two were arrested but one managed to hide inside the school. The armed police entered Ōtāhuhu College. King's College, which was near Ōtāhuhu College, went into lockdown as well, as a precautionary measure. But there was no one hiding inside King's College.

Throughout the morning the *New Zealand Herald* continues writing about the lockdown at King's College. I am scavenging through the news to find something on Ōtāhuhu College. When I finally do, it is a sentence at most. In one article, the *New Zealand Herald* adds details about the establishment of King's College and quotes from concerned parents and students at King's College.

The media is using the lockdown at Ōtāhuhu College as an opportunity to promote King's College. Who cares when King's College was founded? There are hundreds of students locked down at Ōtāhuhu College in fear of a man running from the police, but the media is not telling us anything about it. No one is speaking to the parents of students at Ōtāhuhu College. All this time I am texting my friends who are distressed.

My closest friends were in our English class as the man ran into the school. Our English classroom's door lock is broken. Ōtāhuhu College is a Decile 1 school. It has little money to put towards repairing our buildings. I cannot stop thinking about what might happen if the man finds my English class. He could get in and hurt my friends. I am spiralling out. My head feels like it is going to burst from the pressure.

There was no way to secure that classroom as the man entered the school. All my friends are vulnerable and unsafe. My friend sends me a video of my English teacher putting a rope through a hole in the door and trying to secure it by tying it to the football gear. They are all defenceless. None of this is in the news. The news is busy being concerned about white kids in the school next door, where nothing is happening. How is King's College's precautionary lockdown dominating the headline of every mainstream news platform? Ōtāhuhu College is lucky to be mentioned at the bottom of the articles.

The two schools are separated by one fence. A fence that I could kick down. But we sit on the opposite ends of the wealth spectrum. Ōtāhuhu College is a Decile 1 state school, one of the poorest schools in the country, and King's College is a Decile 10 school, one of the richest and most prestigious schools. The difference between the wealth at Ōtāhuhu College and King's College is so drastic, the kids at King's College are possibly receiving more pocket money than the teachers' pay at my school. Importantly, over 60% of King's College students are Pākehā compared with less than 1% of Ōtāhuhu College students.

The media spends all morning documenting nothingness at King's College, and when King's College gets the clear, the issue is no longer the headline and slips to the bottom of the pile. The imaginary threat to King's College gets more media attention than the real threat in Ōtāhuhu College. The media makes a consistent effort to portray brown South Aucklanders as reckless criminals. It doesn't surprise me when they deem the Māori, Pacific and Asian students at Ōtāhuhu College unworthy of protection. We aren't even considered worthy of attention. It is shocking to New Zealand that something like this could happen at King's College, but it would not have been shocking if the media told the country what really happened.

I have lived in South Auckland ever since my arrival in 2014, and I have never failed to notice how the media associate the brown and poor South Auckland with criminality. Articles name South Auckland if something bad happened here but would never mention the region if it happened in the North Shore. *Police Ten 7* compound this by racially profiling brown people in the region. The media portrays the white students at King's College as victims of violence, though no students are harmed. Brown students at poor South Auckland schools often get portrayed as the perpetrators of violence and never the victims. Plenty of students at Ōtāhuhu College were traumatised. The fear of the students is neither acknowledged nor addressed. It is the battle of the kings and the commoners. The media assumes the role of Kings' protector. Brown students are forced to grow up and look after ourselves, and that comes at the cost of our wellbeing.

High school gets more contentious with time. I do my Year 13 English speech on why trans women should be allowed to participate in women's sports. This is not a popular idea. Things are not getting better at high school. My biology teacher is aware of my English speech. One day during class, unprovoked, she puts a picture of Laurel Hubbard on the TV and screams, 'THAT IS A MAN!' and begins to laugh. I am shocked. I freeze for a moment. I don't know how far she will take it this time. I am lucky that I am in a class of decent students, and no one laughs with the teacher. I am the only openly queer student in that class. I know my teacher is targeting me. It pushes me back into the closet. I have known these people for five years and they still don't accept me for who I am, so how can I trust the world to? I become more and more desperate to leave high school.

But the rebellious spark is still very much alive in me. It has only been a few months since I was refused the title of Prefect in Year

12. I never received a proper explanation for that choice. There are no criteria set out for the selection of prefects either. I am angry, but I know my anger will only give them ammunition to use against me. I walk into the principal's office and demand that he set out criteria for the selection of the Dux. He does. The student who tops the most papers will be named Dux at the end of Year 13. I am not concerned about the award, just the principle. I've grown up having so much of my life controlled by others, and I am putting my foot down on this issue. I am taking back control.

At the end of that year, I become the Dux of Ōtāhuhu College.

15
In the mood
for sex

My last year at high school is already an eventful year. I am not expecting anything else to top it, but things change dramatically when Amanda Ashley, a trans woman living in the Kaipara ki Mahurangi electorate, together with Young Labour and Young Greens, petitions the Labour, New Zealand First and Greens Government to ban conversion therapy. The petition collects over 20,000 signatures. However, banning conversion therapy doesn't become a government policy. Labour list Member of Parliament (MP) Marja Lubeck accepts the petition and puts a member's bill named Prohibition of Conversion Therapy Bill into the member's ballot in 2018.

Member's bills are bills introduced by MPs who are not ministers. They draft a bill, and a number is attached to it. There are approximately 70 member's bills in the biscuit-tin ballot at a time. When a space on the Order Paper becomes available, a ballot is held to decide which member's bill will be introduced. A number is drawn from a biscuit tin, and whichever bill matches the number is introduced to Parliament for first reading. The odds of Marja's bill being drawn from the biscuit tin are 1 in 70.

At the same time, members of Parliament start looking for youth

MPs to represent them at the ninth Youth Parliament in 2019. I apply to represent my local MP Jenny Salesa and Manukau East (Ōtāhuhu, Papatoetoe and Ōtara) at Youth Parliament 2019. I apply to be a part of the youth delegation to the Open Government Partnership Conference in Canada. I don't know much about the Open Government Partnership, but it includes a fully paid trip to Canada with other young people. I haven't travelled outside the Pacific.

My campaign to become a youth MP is built around youth mental health. I don't think that banning conversion therapy is something I can campaign on. Jenny and my local board member, Christine O'Brien, are impressed with my speech and select me as Jenny's youth MP.

I become a youth MP just after Marja introduces her member's bill. The movement to ban conversion therapy has stalled. The new and exciting days of this movement are over. People have heard of it, and many are sick of it. The lack of action that follows the petitions and member's bill leaves people feeling helpless. It appears that things will remain this way for many years.

I am facing problems of my own while trying to become involved in the movement to ban conversion therapy. When trying to apply for university in 2019, I find out that I am classified as an international student. I want to study engineering, but the university fee is $40,000 per year for an international student. My family cannot afford this. There is a view that all international students are extremely wealthy and can afford to pay large sums of money to study. That is not the case for my family. We have no money. My parents have put all their money into renewing our visas to remain in New Zealand and now it seems as though our visas will not be renewed. Our passports have been sitting with Immigration forever, and although my parents never show it, they are afraid.

My education is on pause and there is no guarantee that I have a future in New Zealand. I am in a dark place again. I thought I had escaped the violence and abuse in Fiji. The idea of living in the same community, if I have to return to Fiji, frightens me. The hurt child in me still hasn't healed. There would also be so much shame in returning to Fiji after failing to settle in New Zealand. I become suicidal again. I would rather be dead than put myself through that again. But I can't tell anyone about how I am feeling.

In the midst of drowning in defeat, I get an email congratulating me on my successful application to the Open Government Partnership youth delegation. My passport is still with New Zealand Immigration. Pa asks our lawyer to retrieve my passport so I can apply for my Canadian visa. I am short on time, only a few days before I have to leave. I am hesitant to apply for the visa. I do not want to spend money applying for the visa without any certainty. Of course, there never is certainty with these things, but the uncertainty mixed with the fear of travelling alone to the other side of the world makes me question if I should go ahead. Pa asks for the passport anyway.

The passport arrives, and I apply for the visa. I hassle the Canadian embassy. Email after email after email, and I still hear nothing back. My hotel and flights are booked. All I need is the visa. A day before I have to leave, I call the embassy and hear nothing back. But I check my online visa application status, and it says approved. I am ecstatic. But my passport is still not here. I sit near my door hoping the courier guy will deliver it. I look through the peephole at every noise.

I hear knocks on my door and run for it. There is the delivery guy in his red and yellow uniform holding a brown paper bag. I know what is in it. I act cool about it. I sign the delivery and run to my room to open it. It is my passport with the stamped visa. I am going to Canada!

I will be travelling through Singapore airport. Before boarding the plane, I make a list of things I will do in Singapore airport, because I have a long stopover. On the list of things *not* to do, I write, 'Don't chew gum, don't litter, don't connect to unsecured Wi-Fi and <u>don't be gay</u>.' I will be thousands of kilometres away from home. I do not want to be arrested and deported, or worse locked up in a shoddy prison. It is a crime to be gay in Singapore. I wear my most boring pair of black pants and a boxy brown jacket. I resolve to be as unappealing as possible. Although I must say this is a very hard task for me.

I have Tinder and Grindr downloaded on my phone. I have a picture of me on both apps. Although I tell myself I will not be gay while transiting through Singapore, I open my dating and hook-up apps. I blame my hormone monster for that. I swipe right on a few accounts on Tinder and browse through some profiles on Grindr. I suddenly remember that while googling the laws on queer people in Singapore, I saw an article that said the police were using Grindr to set up hook-ups with gay men and arresting them. I close all my apps at once.

There are men patrolling the airport with guns — I am not going to take any chances. Every time a man with a gun in a camouflage uniform walks by, my anxiety spikes. I think they are coming for me. I slide further and further down in my chair. I stop walking through the airport and remain in my seat outside my terminal door. When I get in the plane out of Singapore, I feel like I have just got out of a war zone.

I arrive in Canada and take a bus to the hotel. It's 3 a.m., but check-in is not till 9 a.m.. I throw myself in the lobby, open Grindr and the homosexual mating call goes off. I scan the lobby to make sure no one is looking. It is too early for anyone to be up.

I get a message from a very cute ginger boy, Théo. He is French.

I reply immediately. We start flirting. I sit on the lobby couch smiling at my phone every time I get a message from him. An hour later, the hotel receptionist lets me into my room. I go straight to bed and do not wake up till midday. I'm supposed to meet with the rest of the youth delegates, but I've woken up late, and it seems they have all gone to see Canada before our meeting later that day. Another delegate, Chaimae, is still at the hotel. Thank God. I do not want to explore Ottawa alone. Chaimae and I do a lot; we take pictures while sitting on monuments, we run into a marathon and barge into a cathedral while the choir is singing. This cathedral is nothing like the chapel in Fiji. I do not fear it. The choir, the light shining through the stained glass and the people praying do not scare me. It is strange for so many reasons. I thought I had built an aversion to religious buildings.

Chaimae and I are the first to get to the meeting that evening. In walks Jordan in a black suit, a blonde sleek low ponytail and clear glasses. The most unbelievable thing happens: I am kind of attracted to her. I look at her, perplexed about why she is so enticing. She is tall, and very masculine. A spanner is thrown in my sexuality. I thought I was gay, and I thought I was attracted only to men, but I get a feeling that may not be the full picture.

Jordan studies at Harvard University. It is trippy to sit next to someone from Harvard for dinner. I speak to her at great length. She starts talking about the importance of queer representation in sports without ever mentioning if she is queer or not. Or maybe she has. I am distracted by the confusion bubbling up in me now. She plays soccer. That explains her Herculean posture. The light bulb goes off in my head. I think I am attracted to masculinity, not men.

I have just told people I am gay. I can't tell them otherwise so quickly after telling them I am confident I am gay. Coming out as bisexual, after coming out gay — I cannot see that going down very well. But I walk to my hotel with a brand-new understanding of my sexuality.

I check Grindr after connecting to the hotel Wi-Fi. I have messages from Théo. Without thinking much, I agree to his request to come over and wait anxiously for him to arrive. He knocks on the door and I play it cool, pretending I have not picked my shorts and t-shirt just for him. He has a moustache. I am into it. I can feel my heartbeat in my head.

I never got to experience lust the way my straight friends did in high school. Queer lust was forbidden. I was not allowed to look at boys for too long because that would somehow imply that I was asking for a beating. I was not allowed to hold hands with the person I adored. I hid everything deep down, my desires, my dreams, my love. I became so lonely. When Théo touches me for the first time, the years of suppressed emotions rush to the surface. It is overwhelming and frighteningly cruel. I freeze and then I feel nauseous.

Although I want to be intimate with Théo, my experience of conversion therapy from five years ago still controls my life so intrinsically. Every time he touches me, my body flinches. I am frustrated and angry. All I can do is cry. It does not make any sense to me. I have escaped the violence. It is years since I needed to be in fight or flight mode, but I am. Is my conversion therapy going to follow me for the rest of my life?

Once I have stopped snapping myself with a rubber band every time I think or feel queerly, the association between pain and queerness weakens, and I learn that queerness itself does not induce pain. I need to surround myself with people who love me for my queerness. With his touches, Théo is disrupting the relationship between pain and queerness that my conversion therapy created. He is becoming a part of my healing without either of us ever knowing it. Every touch is a revolutionary act of queer healing. It is a revolutionary act to be our true selves in a world that is not okay with our existence. Théo makes me realise that accepting that I am queer could be a beautiful experience. After every touch, I feel better. I feel prouder. I feel happier. He is teaching me that I am deserving of love and that love should never hide in fear.

We spend the first night cuddling. I am too nervous to do anything more and he realises that. He is sweet and kind and caring and patient. In a few days, we are all over each other. It feels like the early days of dating, when your hearts are racing and your fingers are competing to message each other. I go to the conference in the day only to rush back to the hotel to hang out with him.

He brings fried chicken. We sit on the bed facing each other. I've just started to grow my hair out. He pushes my hair back with his right hand, tickling my face. He leans in and asks, 'May I?' I take a deep breath in, drop my head down and lean in. He lifts my chin with his left hand, cupping my face with his right. He starts playing with my earring, twisting the stud in my freshly pierced ear. My neck squirms like a worm out of pain.

'Does it hurt?' he asks.

'A little,' I respond. He stops. His face travels close to my mine.

'Is this okay?' he asks again, trying to comfort me.

'Yes,' I say. I feel his seductive breath on my face. He kisses my shoulder, and my body twitches. He runs his lips up my neck and before making it to my ear, he bites me gently. I want more.

He knows what he is doing. Me? Not so much. I moan as he kisses my neck. He stops and looks in my eyes. His eyes exude patience and safety. He places my left hand on his chest. I can feel warmth blossom there. I place my right hand on the back of his head. My forehead joins his. We roll our faces up. Our noses meet first, and then our lips. His lips are soft but his moustache rough.

He presses his cushion lips on my disproportionately large ones. I part my lips ever so slightly, allowing his tongue to slip inside. I close my eyes, and the warmth consumes us.

He pushes me down on the bed and I fumble to take off my shirt. He pulls my pants down. I rip his clothes off like the underwear package I bought from Jack's. We lie in bed bare. His finger brushes my nipples and turns me on. I feel his warm body above me. He caresses my thighs as he begins to slowly thrust inside me.

Our hearts thud as one. Our bodies press together, the heat nearly melting us into one. He is moving faster now. He holds my hand firmly, pressing his impossibly soft lips on mine. I start to enjoy the feel of his coarse moustache. He rests his body on his right elbow, slides his hands behind my head and gently pulls my hair. I release all my stress in a moan.

Time goes by quickly. We are meant to hang out on my last night in Canada. Chaimae insists that I attend the conference closing party with her. Chaimae physically drags me with her. I regret it immediately. I spend every moment at the party thinking about Théo in a room filled with people who do not know what it feels like to live in a world that forbids your love. I wake the next morning and make my way to the airport. Théo video-calls me while I am waiting to board my flight. Tears well up as I board the plane to New Zealand. I cry like Elio cried when Oliver left him in *Call Me By Your Name*.

I can finally look in the mirror and tell myself that I am queer. I am queer like the sky is blue and grass is green. I am queer like the summer is hot and the winter is cold. I am queer because I have survived. I am queer because I am strong. I am queer because I am not ashamed. I am queer because I refuse to live a lie. I am deeply and relentlessly queer.

16
Fighter

My eyes are bulging into tomatoes from the crying. I cover my eyes with the airline sleep mask. While I was in Canada attending the Open Government Partnership conference, my family's New Zealand residence visa is approved. I arrive back at Auckland Airport to the very welcome news. It is a relief.

As an Asian, I could be four things: a doctor, a teacher, an engineer or a failure. I enrol into engineering for Semester 2, but I regret it as soon as the classes start. I enrolled in engineering because I'd done calculus and physics in high school and I was good at it, but I sucked at engineering. When the lecturer showed us an electrical board, I cried out of boredom.

It was a long, tough journey to get into university. Now that I am in, there is no way out. I am miserable for an entire week. I am the smartest kid in my family, so why do I struggle so much with engineering? I'm not meant to struggle! I stick around for another week, and it makes me so depressed, I am constantly crying.

South Asian kids do not drop out of school. It is out of the question. There is so much shame associated with it. My aunties will taunt Ma if I drop out of university. They will taunt her about how the smartest kid in the family was not smart enough for university. I am a failure. I have failed at engineering.

No matter how much shame I feel, the depressing nature of studying engineering outweighs it. I muster the courage and tell

Ma that I am dropping out of engineering and enrolling into law and arts degrees. I am going to major in psychology in my arts degree. I am too late to enrol in psychology for 2019, so I can't start university till 2020. To my surprise, Ma is not mad at all. I have been overthinking, but a weight is lifted off my chest now. Dropping out of school is a ground-breaking thing for me to do in my family.

Youth Parliament kicks off on 15 July 2019. It is a daunting event filled with elitist Pākehā youth. Ala Vailala, Youth MP for the Honourable Aupito William Sio, and I become good friends. We are two of very few Pacific youth MPs. We look after each other. Youth Parliament is a two-day event. The first day has question time from youth MPs to ministers of government in the morning and select committee in the afternoon. The second day is for the general debates. I am allocated three minutes in the general debate.

On the morning of my speech, before Ala and I leave our hotel, I blast 'Never Knew Love Like this Before' by Stephanie Mills and have a dance in Ala's room. Yes, we are youth MPs, but we are also young. I don't want to miss out on key years of my youth because I entered politics too young. Brown young people from lows-socioeconomic communities are forced to grow up quickly. We feel the pressure to support our families financially. My friends and I gave up our hobbies to assist our families or to take care of our educational needs. If it isn't poverty forcing us to grow up, it's the external pressures that train us to behave like grown-ups. Anything negative I do is taken to represent all brown people, but rarely ever are my achievements seen as the fruits of the labour of my community.

The pressure on Ala and me to represent two of the most impoverished Pacific-dominated electorates, Māngere and Manukau East, is high. We are held to a higher standard than the Pākehā youth MPs. A Pākehā youth MP took pictures with people wearing MAGA hats and pulling the Hitler salute and went on to become a National party candidate. Meanwhile, Metiria Turei was bullied into resigning after it was revealed she lied to claim benefits twenty years earlier as a single mother. Israel Folau was immediately cancelled for making homophobic comments, while the likes of Simon O'Connor and Judith Collins are still popular National MPs after making several transphobic remarks. My brown friends and I have to be squeaky clean. Once we are in the public eye, the act is on. Code switched. That's why we dance in our room. It is crucial for us to curate joy while existing in white institutions.

I've been going back and forth about the topic for my speech. Maybe I should speak about youth mental health? That is a popular topic. No. I should talk about racism. That will surely get everyone's attention. Something in me knows that neither of these topics are right. Youth Parliament presents itself as the golden opportunity to put life back into the movement to ban conversion therapy.

I'm not sure how the other youth MPs or the country will respond to me. I have come to know New Zealand as a dangerous place for queer people, but I am hoping that young people will be different.

In the evening towards the end of the general debate, the speaker says, 'I call Shaneel Shavneel Lal.'

With my heart beating harder than ever, my palms drenched in sweat and my voice shaking, I stand up:

> Mr Speaker, when I woke up this morning, I didn't look in the mirror and say, 'Oops, I'm gay, better fix that,' . . .

The house erupts in laughter. Suddenly, I am in my element. I continue, more confidently this time:

> because like any rational person, I know my sexuality was not a choice.

But the years of compulsory heterosexuality have caused me so much confusion, and while we live in a system of institutionalised heteronormativity, my human rights are still not a human reality.

Thirty-three years ago, homosexuality was a crime; six years ago, same-sex marriage was illegal; but to this day, it is completely legal to torture someone to change their sexuality in the name of conversion therapy. To the heterosexual people in this room, how many times have you been asked, 'What caused your heterosexuality?' or, 'Have you considered conversion therapy to overcome your heterosexual desires?' Probably never.

In New Zealand, conversion therapy is not a mainstream but a pseudoscientific treatment, and there are no professional standards for how it is conducted. In fact, it is now widely practised by religious organisations to push forward their bigoted agenda. These people believe that homosexuality is a choice or a result of some childhood trauma.

In the '60s, conversion therapy included giving patients nausea-inducing drugs while showing them same-sex pornography. Recent tactics include electroconvulsive therapy where an electric shock induces a seizure causing memory loss. Now, some have turned to psychoanalysis where young people are hammered with the idea that homosexuality is a disease and told to pray to God to heal them.

I am reminded of the story of the young Australian boy, Chris, who was only sixteen when his church introduced him to conversion therapy. He was so ashamed and guilt-ridden, he says he prayed to God to 'heal him or kill him'. *Heal him or kill him.* Make no mistake, conversation therapy is not about 'praying the gay away', it's about mentally torturing the most vulnerable to death. Mainstream psychologists say this therapy is ineffective, unethical and harmful.

In October 2018, Marja Lubeck introduced a bill into the member's bill ballot proposing a ban on conversion therapy. I urge members of Parliament to get behind this bill and ban conversion therapy. As a politician, it is your job to alleviate the collective suffering of your people, and if you allow this torture to continue, you are failing your people.

We are not broken, and we do not need to be fixed.

Standing in Parliament after finishing my speech is the most vulnerable moment of my teenage years. I've opened my heart and let it bleed for the country to see. Aotearoa is seeing a strong and brave young person fighting for the betterment of our country, but I am broken and weak. I haven't healed from my conversion therapy. I haven't healed from being told that I was broken and needed to be fixed. I haven't healed from being beaten for existing.

My identity becomes wrapped around trying to protect other vulnerable queer people. I don't realise that every setback in the movement to end such 'therapy' will start to feel like a personal failure. While protecting queer people brings me peace, the process of banning conversion therapy is violent to me.

I am fired up. I feel the same amount of passion in this moment as I did when I was standing up against Jack. This time I am prepared and confident. When I stood up against Jack, I felt unsafe and afraid. I retaliated against his hatred without knowing how to deal with it. I was vulnerable, unaware of my power and voice. I no longer feel afraid. I feel powerful. That scared teenager in me is dead. There is no point in trying to hide. Safety was never guaranteed for me. It doesn't matter whether I am hidden or not.

Every person who hurt me was preparing me for this day. My true self has arrived at Youth Parliament, and boy, it is a grand entrance! I suddenly find a purpose in life beyond just surviving. I thought my life would begin and end trying to hide my true self, but now I have a powerful voice, and I can use that voice to fight back. For a broken, beaten-down kid, this moment feels liberating. I no longer see myself as a victim, I see a fighter.

I have always been a part of the queer legacy, but it is only in this moment that I realise I belong in the queerhood made up of generations of queer people showing revolutionary resistance. My conversion therapy prevented me from finding other people like me. It isolated me from my people. But I belong in my community, I have a role to play. As I stand at my seat in the Youth Parliament I feel the presence of my ancestors. Years of colonisation and criminalisation forced my queer ancestors into hiding. It is time for them to live through my existence. They watch over me as I speak, each word bringing me closer to them. This is *our* battle. I am only the medium through which we are all about to fight.

There is only so much I can say at Youth Parliament. I leave the politicians with a message — 'As politicians it is your duty to alleviate the collective suffering of your people, and if you allow this torture to continue, you are failing your people.' There is a standing ovation in the house after my speech. This speech puts our fight back on the country's agenda.

On the day of my speech Marja is watching from the gallery. Our friendship and co-activism to ban conversion therapy begins in this moment. We look at each other as the Parliament erupts in applause, and we both know that we are going on a long journey together.

I upload my speech to Instagram and Facebook and within the first hour it goes viral. Many people don't know that conversion therapy is legal in New Zealand. Others refuse to believe this is a real issue for the queer community. The support floods in, but so do the death threats. One person says, 'Go hang yourself'. Another says, 'Go to Hell'. The right-wing conservatives and Christian extremists are furious with me. How dare I have the audacity to stand up for my rights? *Newshub* writes, 'Youth MP's call for gay conversion therapy ban exposes homophobic underbelly.' But there is no homophobic *underbelly*. Homophobia and transphobia are rampant. The media ignore it till it becomes deadly. Green MP Golriz Ghahraman and the New Zealand Parliament tweet their support. I am getting a real taste of being in the public eye as an outspoken marginalised person. For many it would serve as a deterrent, but for me it is encouragement to go all the way with this movement. The movement to ban conversion therapy is on!

I find myself leading the biggest queer rights movement of my time in Aotearoa. I have all eyes on me following Youth Parliament, and I have to capitalise on that attention.

Multiple people express to me that they want to work with me to ban conversion therapy. I have no experience organising a campaign. I tap into the people who've reached out. I contact Neihana Waitai, Max Tweedie, Harry Robson and Shannon Novak and create a Facebook group chat. This is the creation of the Conversion Therapy Action Group, which soon comes to be known as CTAG. We think about calling our group Action on Conversion

Therapy (ACT), but I'd rather conversion therapy be legal than be mistaken for David Seymour. We commit to CTAG.

I found CTAG to consistently advocate for a ban on conversion therapy. Our role expands with time — we start to engage religious groups, student bodies, medical organisations, mental health organisations and human rights organisations. The work multiplies itself into a mammoth. While we are in the public domain presenting the case to ban conversion therapy, we are also scattering to gather research and data around it. We have to present ourselves as though we have everything figured out, but the reality is that we are discovering things as the movement progresses. It is go, go, go. When we are met with opposition, we discuss over days as a group on how to respond to it. This becomes very common practice for CTAG. It is how our movement develops.

When a petition is submitted for a select committee to consider, the select committee must meet and respond to it. The first two petitions to ban conversion therapy were submitted on 8 August 2018 and 14 September 2018. They were accepted but set aside. They aren't of interest anymore. CTAG is on it. We start making noise on social media and in the news about the lack of response from the Justice Select Committee.

What the Justice Select Committee reports back in October 2019 shocks us. They fail to recommend a ban on conversion therapy. The Justice Select Committee is made up of four Labour MPs: Meka Whaitiri, Ginny Andersen, Clare Curran and Greg O'Connor, and four National MPs: Tim Macindoe, Mark Mitchell, Chris Penk and Nick Smith. This select committee states overtly that practising conversion therapy, an abusive practice that pushes queer people into depression and suicide, is protected by freedom of religion. The report reads:

It would also be a challenge to determine which practices should be defined as conversion therapy and which should be legitimate activities for religious and other groups.

The Bill of Rights Act affirms, protects, and promotes human rights and fundamental freedoms in New Zealand. It allows all New Zealanders to live free from discrimination, including in relation to their sexual orientation. New Zealanders also have the right to freedom of religion. This protects those who offer and seek out conversion therapy because of their religious views.

Infuriated, I take to Instagram to announce that the Justice Select Committee is bootlicking and pandering to religious bigots.

I am in despair. They don't understand the gravity of the torment I went through and that others put into conversion therapy go through for them to sit there and advocate for conversion therapy in the name of freedom of religion. Religious leaders forced me into a place where I believed that I would be better off dead than queer. I spent my childhood hating myself for who I was. I didn't understand my queerness, but I knew it was something that disgusted everyone around me. I begged to God to change me and when that didn't happen, I became more depressed and the punishment from the religious leaders became more extreme.

The Justice Select Committee are protecting my abusers but disregarding my safety. It has been five years since I escaped conversion therapy in Fiji, but the wounds are still fresh.

The report concludes:

We agree with the argument that conversion therapy is harmful. However, we believe more work needs to be done

125

before any decision is taken to ban it. In particular, thought must be given to how to define conversion therapy, who the ban would apply to, and how to ensure that rights relating to freedom of expression and religion were maintained.

The Justice Select Committee report is defeating. Labour and National have taken a stance and it isn't in favour of queer people. They spend more words in their report arguing that religious people's right to practise conversion therapy is protected under religious freedoms than they spend condemning conversion therapy and defending the lives of queer people. What they conveniently forget to mention is that no rights in New Zealand are absolute. They speak so much of the New Zealand Bill of Rights while forgetting to mention section 5, which reads:

The rights and freedoms contained in this Bill of Rights may be subject only to such reasonable limits prescribed by law as can be demonstrably justified in a free and democratic society.

Religious rights are not absolute and sure as hell are not a justification to abuse queer people. Protecting people from religious abuse is a justifiable limitation on religious freedom. If you have to balance a religious right against someone's humanity, that religious right should not exist.

The only time freedom of religion is invoked in this country is in the name of hatred and bigotry. It is never invoked to protect queer people. The only time the elders used religion was to convert me. They never used it to nurture me. Christian extremists pick and choose when it suits them to be religious and godly, and when it does not, they simply abandon it. If a religion teaches someone to hate people, to abuse children, then that religion is the problem, and that god is not all-loving.

We have our work cut out for us. David Seymour is very clear that he will not support the ban on conversion therapy. New Zealand First refuses to give a position. The majority of Parliament is leaving queer people to fend for ourselves. The only party supporting a ban on conversion therapy is the Green party, but they don't have nearly enough numbers to ban it. The queer community is defeated by the Justice Select Committee's report. We thought Labour would have our back but instead, they turn their backs on us.

I become popular overnight after my speech at Youth Parliament.

One night a man I've been talking to, Tyler, messages me and asks to see me. I agree. He says he will come around and pick me up by eight. He wants to go on a drive. I wait and wait, and he is nowhere to be seen. I message him to no replies. I am about to go to bed when he calls me. It is past midnight, and he is outside my house. I am annoyed at him, but I can't refuse to see him. I mean, the guy is parked outside my house.

I sneak out of my house. Ma is asleep and Pa at work. I get in his car, and he launches into an explanation for his tardiness. I do not pay it much mind. I can smell his breath. He is drunk. I am immediately annoyed. I tell him he needs to park his car on the road and get a taxi home, but he is not listening to a word I say. He drives us down the road away from my house.

I thought he would sweet-talk me. My brows furrow, and my forehead wrinkles. I frown like fury. We do not exchange any words. He looks angry. His eyes are red, and his breath hot and heavy. He puts his hand on my chest and pushes me back into my seat. Like a white family in a horror movie, I've walked into the monster. I resist his push and try to lean forward. But he slides my seat back, turns the car off and leans over me with all his body. I can feel the pressure of his upper body on me. He leans in for a kiss, and I turn my face away. He grabs my face firmly by the chin and moves it to face him. I push back. He grabs my face again, more aggressively this time. I move his hand off my chin and in fury, he slams me back in my seat and leans my seat down.

My body enters a state of shock. I hold my breath, my throat dries and shrinks, and my limbs become numb.

He starts kissing me on my neck. My neck jerks in protest. He places his hand on my throat to hold me still. He kisses me on my lips, before going back down to bite my neck. I use all the power in my body to push myself up. It is not enough to get me up, but just the right amount to outrage Tyler. He takes aim at my chest with his fist and cements me to the seat.

My surroundings become static for a moment. The pain shoots up like fire in my chest. I wince in pain, and then I'm stiff in fear of Tyler. He places his hand on my throat again, this time choking me. He wraps his hand tightly enough around my neck to make my eyes bulge and bites my bottom lip. Then he slaps me across my face.

When he lets go of my neck, I jump out of my seat, fighting for my breath. I am reduced to tears. Tyler is not letting go anytime soon. He presses me back into my seat and takes a shot at my left shoulder. It hurts like my entire arm is stuck in an electrical barbed wire. My left hand is useless now, but I am still determined to fight. I take my right hand to his face, but he avoids my hand like an expert. He crunches his fist in my right shoulder and discharges punches like bullets in my body.

He gropes me, waiting for a reaction. He's rendered me useless. It is clear that I am not going to get away from him, and if I try, he will kill me. He grabs the waistband of my shorts and boxers and begins to pull them down. I struggle to keep them on, but he takes them off in a matter of seconds.

There is a blank stare on my face as my head bops back and forth. I try to breathe to minimise the pain, but nothing helps. It feels never-ending. When he is done, he leans away. He tells me to leave as I lie in the car seat paralysed. He opens the door and pushes me out. I drag myself into the house. He has violated me. Tyler has looted every bit of freedom Théo and I so passionately fought for. I am no longer free. Tyler's actions suffocate me and cage me in my head. I lie in bed, numb, staring at the ceiling.

I consider speaking out against him, but I realise no one would believe me. It is my word against his.

I have been accused of being an activist for attention. I have no doubt I will be accused of lying about being assaulted for attention. I am queer and brown — the odds are not in my favour. I am being watched by the media after Youth Parliament. Any mishap on my part could affect the movement to ban conversion therapy. I cannot tell anyone.

I call Frederic. I feel broken. Frederic and I did not work out, but we never stopped talking. Tyler had a profoundly destructive impact on me. Frederic is gentle, kind, protective and nurturing. He is everything that I need at this point. Frederic helps me get out of the darkest place in my life.

Tyler violated me. He made me hate my body. On many days I do not get out of bed. I do not brush or eat. I lie in bed incapacitated. Frederic helps me return to my body after a long time of feeling like a stranger to it. We haven't got over each other. He still has not come out to his family. Being so close to him after what happened to me rekindles our attachment to each other. Frederic is the only man I feel safe with.

We start spending a lot more time together. We spend a lot of time at the movies, where we are hidden from the world, and at his apartment in the city. We spend a lot of time lying around, my body stacked on his. We enjoy each other's presence, and we look good together. Our relationship is blossoming by the day.

Frederic has noticeably changed. He was once hard to keep up with. Now he has an untroubled calmness and serenity about him. He never acts on impulse, or anger. I am quite the opposite. I am easy to rile and upset. I allow people to get to me easily. But I know to never take my anger out on Frederic. The angelic boy would never fight back. He manages to calm me down, though. To my Instagram followers, I am tough as nails. Frederic knows I am a sensitive cry-baby.

The things that bothered me about Frederic are still there, but I learn to accept them. I'm not perfect either. He is still private about his feelings, his thoughts. I struggle if I do not know everything. I assume the worst. I should never be left to fill in the blanks, I fill them in with the most petrifying thoughts.

17

Mr Gay New Zealand

Mr Gay New Zealand. There is so much infatuated craziness around it. But I don't mind. It is a way to make some queer friends and stop feeling like an outlier in the queer community. I also have very little experience of being in spaces that celebrate my queerness. I jump with joy at the idea of a competition that revolves around celebrating queer excellence and leadership. Perhaps I'm vain and superficial, but that is permissible after all I've been through.

The purpose of Mr Gay New Zealand is to find a leader in the queer community. My activism has hit a roadblock. I am feeling defeated by the Justice Select Committee's recommendation to not ban conversion therapy. I feel that many queer people are relying on me to do something about it. That expectation to somehow overturn the Justice Select Committee's recommendation is unrealistic, but most do not see reason. They see that I am failing to counter the MPs.

I still do not have many connections to politicians or the media, and I struggle to bring attention back to banning conversion therapy. I have exhausted my passion and drive floundering to keep the movement alive. My energy is depleted. I desire euphoria. When the applications for Mr Gay New Zealand 2020 open, I apply in haste believing I can use the competition to reignite the flames.

I start exploring queer spaces to find people like me, only to end up feeling like I am the only instance of colour happening in all the queer spaces I enter. I am trying to understand why the queer community, especially its leaders, are so white. I can find queer people, but I can't find queer people who look like me. Maybe I can change the face of the queer community by entering Mr Gay New Zealand.

I am delighted when I receive the email to confirm that I have made it to the finals of Mr Gay New Zealand. I think everyone who applies makes it to the finals, though. I start planning my outfits and campaign. The competition has six categories: writing an opinion piece, completing an interview with the judges, sitting a test on queer history, fundraising at the Big Gay Out, public speaking and a public vote. The rule, as I understand, has always been that whoever wins the most categories automatically wins the title of Mr Gay New Zealand. I know my strengths are in campaigning for the public vote, writing and public speaking. I start studying for the test early.

There is no limitation on what could be tested so I try to study as widely as I can. Which country decriminalised homosexuality first? Who was the first to allow same-sex marriage? Which year did the riots at Stonewall take place? Who founded the New Zealand AIDS Foundation? How can you contract or pass on HIV AIDS? How often should you get tested? My brain is dripping with queer history.

Mr Gay New Zealand finalists and judges are all added to a Facebook group chat. Mr Gay New Zealand started in 2009, and the title consistently went to a white gay man till 2016, when it was won by an Asian person. The judges tell me that was the year they stopped treating Mr Gay New Zealand like a beauty contest. In the eleven years that the Mr Gay New Zealand competition has been running, only one non-European person of colour has won the title.

The default race for queerness is white until proven otherwise. The default race for Mr Gay New Zealand feels white to me too.

The competition truly begins when the public voting opens. I never question my ability to win public vote. Although it is only some 5000 followers big, my online community loves me very much. I become the fan favourite finalist for Mr Gay New Zealand. Siteri's mum gifts me her *ngatu* (tapa cloth) to wear for the competition. My cousins Neha and Reha and I go to Murphy Park in Ōtāhuhu and photograph me in the *ngatu*. I am strutting across Murphy Park in conservative Ōtāhuhu without any concern for what people think of me or would do to me. I feel joy, and even though I don't have an audience, I feel the presence of my ancestors. For a moment I am removed from the physical realm and connected to the spiritual realm. And my community has felt it too. I've led the public vote category from the beginning of the competition. The Pacific community rallies to put me ahead of the other contestants.

I am getting distracted by the glamourous façade of the competition. It is an adrenaline rush. As an immigrant I was taught that the only thing I had to offer was my labour. My self-worth was built around what I could produce. In fact, my self-worth was intrinsically dependent on my achievements. Now that I've stopped working all the time to compete in something as frivolous as Mr Gay New Zealand, I can no longer cope with the foreboding uneasiness.

I am used to working endlessly and when I don't, I experience severe productivity anxiety. Every time I stop working, take a break or try to peacefully enjoy a moment, my anxiety peaks to a debilitating level. I feel like I am never doing enough or that others are always doing more than me and working harder than me. I feel like I am lazy and wasteful with my time. No matter how many hours I work or how much work I finish, I am never at ease or satisfied. I set myself unrealistic goals and I struggle to sleep when I don't achieve them. I develop a habit of skipping breakfast. I need to optimise every hour of my day.

Fun, joy, happiness — all these things trigger my productivity anxiety. I was taught as a kid that feeling these emotions often meant I was compromising how much time I had for work. I put off all the things that made me feel good. I put off anything that made me feel at all. I saw feeling emotions and working through them as a waste of my time. I feel unworthy of having positive feelings.

I haven't resolved my survivor's guilt. I am safe physically, but my mind is in survival mode long after it doesn't have to be. I made it out of conversion therapy, but my friends did not, and that haunts me every day. I feel I don't deserve good things and I don't know how to deal with that feeling. How dare I be happy while the people who supported me through the toughest days of my life are still suffering? I suppress happiness and kick it to the side. I joined Mr Gay New Zealand with a purpose. I have to find a way to bring the country's attention back to banning conversion therapy.

The Pride march takes place a day before the Big Gay Out in 2020. On the morning of the march, I arrive at the New Zealand AIDS Foundation building in St Marys Bay and wait outside for others. Soon all the contestants and the judges are there. This is the main day of the competition. We are getting photographed, interviewed, tested and making a public-speaking appearance at Family Bar at midnight. I have prepared thoroughly for every category, but things don't go as I planned.

On the first day of the event, *Married at First Sight* contestant Ray Wedlake and I protest the name of the competition. We both find the title 'Mr Gay' too limiting and unrepresentative of the queer community. We ask for something more inclusive of the trans and nonbinary community but are told by the judges that trans people are already competing despite the name not including them. I don't strictly feel like a boy. I don't have the words to communicate how I feel but I am coming to terms with my gender fluidity. But I think that to win Mr Gay New Zealand I have to maintain the image of a cisgender gay man. Winners in the past have been masculine cisgender men, and when the judges push back against making the title more inclusive, it affirms my suspicion that if I am anything but a cis-gay man I will be treated as less than in the world. I am not thinking of the competition. I am hiding my true self. In many ways I am too hopeful and optimistic that I can change the power structure in the queer community.

I am the last person to be interviewed. There are four white and two brown gay men interviewing us. During my interview, one of the judges asks how I would feel about becoming Mr Gay Fiji if I do not win Mr. Gay New Zealand. I find that a strange thing to say to me seconds into my interview for Mr Gay New Zealand. Why would I be Mr Gay Fiji? I don't live in Fiji, and I am not being voted for by Fijians. I live in New Zealand, and New Zealanders are voting for me to represent them. I would do a disservice to Fijians if I took the title of Mr Gay Fiji. I live in the diaspora, and I am not connected enough to them to represent them. White gay New Zealanders have no right to choose who gets to represent Fiji. I decline his offer.

I am prepared to talk about my aspirations and dreams for the queer community. I want to show the judges what I have already achieved for the community, and what else I can do, but it seems they are not interested in that. The questioning begins and I start to get frustrated. They ask me why I am so aggressive. They ask me if I can find a balance between aggression and passion. They question whether I have the right temperament to be Mr Gay New Zealand.

They only know me through my speech at Youth Parliament. My opinion piece for the competition was about banning conversion therapy, but I am not getting any questions about the movement to ban conversion therapy. The questioning reminds me of the moment I was standing in my high school principal's office listening to him say I was too extroverted and flamboyant to be a prefect. These excuses are feeble. This doesn't feel like an interview; it feels like a defended hearing. I am the defendant and the white gay men have appointed themselves to the bench.

While the white contestants are being asked about what they hope to achieve for the community, I am being forced to defend myself. White queer people are not put through a process of character vetting to determine whether they are fit for the title of Mr Gay New Zealand.

The reality is that the judges have no evidence of me being aggressive or angry. I feel like they are trying to create evidence. I feel pushed to my limits. I find these questions outrageous. If I respond aggressively I fear I will give them evidence of the supposed anger I have. I have valid reason to be angry. They have, unprovoked, started to make allegations of aggressiveness against me without any evidence. They have construed all the work I have done towards banning conversion therapy as aggression. I'm not falling for it. I am determined not to snap. If these men can reasonably paint me as an aggressive brown man, they will be justified to cancel me in the competition.

This is what happens to anyone who retaliates against the status quo. White men enforce decorum, civility, kindness and respectability to maintain the white status quo. These standards of respectability, kindness, civility and decorum are the creations of white men. They help white men to maintain control and hold power over all people. Anyone who questions the status quo is painted as aggressive, unkind and incapable of maintaining decorum, and that justifies cancelling them. That is what is going to happen to me if I retaliate against their line of questioning. There is nothing civil and kind about what they are doing to me. There is nothing kind or civil about how white men come into power. There is nothing civil about the colonisation and genocide of indigenous people. They want to impose standards of decorum and civility against the people they've stepped on to get into power.

Underlying all of these judges' questions is the message that, you, Shaneel, scare us. I am not going to change the face of the queer community by acquiescing to the staus quo. I need to frighten them. A leader that doesn't terrify the status quo is not going to change it. There is a turmoil in me. The radical in me wants to thump the table and leave the competition. The little queer kid in me wants to win the competition and get some validation. This is my first proper chance to introduce myself to the queer community in person. I will feel less lonely if I can convince some queer people to like me. I allow the broken child in me to make my decisions. I leave my interview feeling powerless.

One of the white gay judges, Elliot, reaches out and apologises to me after the interview, but it is too late. No one stood up for me during the interview. Only I had my back. He quietly let other white people carry out their interrogation only to reach out after the harm was done. His apology means nothing.

After we've all been interviewed, we sit a test on queer history. I am confident I'll do well, since I now know my history thoroughly. We then make our way to the Pride march — a different type of event now than the one I participated in in 2018. Last year, in 2019, the Auckland Pride Board banned the police from marching in the Pride parade in uniform after queer people expressed they felt unsafe with the heavy police presence. Queer people of colour and trans people in particular raised concerns about the New Zealand Police's racist and transphobic pattern of behaviour. The decision was controversial, and a number of major sponsors withdrew financial support from the Auckland Pride Festival because of it. To them, police being able to attend the Pride parade in uniform was more important than queer people of colour and trans people feeling safe. They thought that because Pride is about inclusivity, we should accept everyone regardless of how they treat queer people. Some argued that queer police should be allowed to attend in their police uniform, though I don't remember any gay police making this argument themselves.

The Auckland Pride Festival offered the police Pride t-shirts. They refused to wear them and pulled out from the parade entirely. It was pure theatrics. If the police truly cared for the safety of the queer community, they would have cooperated. Instead, they equated their uniform to our identity. Being a police officer is a job, not an identity. The police take their uniform off every time they are off duty. Queer people of colour are never off duty. We cannot skin ourselves at the end of each day. We do not get to take our skin off when we are tired of racism. We do not get to quit our identity. This is our life, and we live in our skin at all times, even when the world is violent to us.

The police failed to uphold their commitments to the queer community. The ban on police uniform gave them an opening to escape accountability for their failures. They could then blame the queer community for being difficult to engage with. The conversation was no longer about the police's failures to meet their commitments to the queer community. It now focused on how a bunch of radical lefties victimised the police and bullied them out of Pride.

A group of predominantly old white gay men formed Rainbow Pride Auckland to create a Pride with police. These men left

Auckland Pride Festival in solidarity with the police. I felt that their allyship to the police overpowered their commitment to protect and serve queer people of colour and trans people.

The white gay men who left the Auckland Pride Festival said they couldn't be racist or transphobic because they were gay and had been criminalised themselves, and their gayness made them immune from racism and transphobia. Some of them didn't consider race as a factor of marginalisation. Their exit made me feel like the consistent advocacy to achieve trans rights and rights for queer people of colour was a step too far.

When the white gay organisers of Rainbow Pride Auckland invited the police to their Pride, it exposed queer people of colour and trans people as the primary group that protested police presence at Pride. They positioned themselves as the peacemakers, which in my view left queer people of colour and trans people framed as the disruptors. In a system of faux decorum and civility, this again allowed white people to cancel queer people of colour and trans people.

When some old white gay men left the Auckland Pride Festival they took with them some of the resources and funding for the Auckland Pride Festival. That is the power that their whiteness afforded them — to control all the resources available to queer people. Most trans people and people of colour were left behind at Auckland Pride Festival with a public fundraiser.

The Pride march in 2020 feels mundane. All the resources have left with the white gay men. My head is filled with dread from Mr Gay New Zealand, and I am looking for a moment of escape, to enjoy myself and forget about the competition. When I arrive at Albert Park, I see people scattered all over the park. It is quieter than usual — there is no music. The voices of the judges are echoing louder in my head than the voices of queer people gathered at

Albert Park.

The absence of music stands out to me. I always loved the noise of the world being drowned out by the loud music at Pride. I danced without pause at the 2018 Pride Parade. I was euphoric, lost in a world of celebration. This year I am confronted by silence. I feel that the community's spirit is low. The battles between young and old queer people, between people of colour and white queer people and between cis and trans folk in the previous year have torn us apart.

I look around Albert Park to see if I can recognise anyone, but being so new to queer spaces, I don't know many people. I don't feel solidarity with my people. The Pride parade in the previous years focused so much on celebration that without the loud music, drag queens singing on trucks and semi-naked men flexing their muscles, the community has no other understanding of coming together and celebrating our resilience and excellence. Pride served as a distraction from homophobia and transphobia for many queer people. With the parade gone, I can feel the heartache of those around me in the park, and it triggers a dire urgency to unify my people. We have forgotten our collective purpose.

In 1972, Ngahuia Te Awekotuku formed the Gay Liberation Movement at the University of Auckland after being denied a visa to study in the United States because she was a lesbian. We come back to Albert Park, behind the University of Auckland, searching for our purpose. I feel *saudade* — a deep nostalgia for collective action. I am convinced the disruption in the queer community is a pivotal moment. Queer and trans people of colour refused to accept racism and transphobia and it reset our community. Walking from Albert Park to Aotea Square, I fear the queer community is lost. The fight to ban conversion therapy is ahead of us and it requires our community to be united and prepared, but instead we are torn apart by racism and transphobia. For a fleeting moment, the stresses of Mr Gay New Zealand escape me and bigger worries engulf me. The fact that I will almost certainly be cheated out of winning seems trivial now.

The Pride march led us to the Pride party in Aotea Square. I pull aside the reigning Mr Gay New Zealand, Nick Francis. I tell him I'm not going to win. I let my emotions out before I have to meet the judges again for the public-speaking part of the competition. After being offered the title of Mr Gay Fiji and the way my interview went, I have more than a gut feeling that I am correct.

Later that night, we go backstage at Family Bar. It is a room full of queens' makeup, costumes and wigs. It is steaming in here. I remove a few layers of clothes to cool down. We make our appearance at Family Bar just before midnight. The question put to us is 'What is your favourite sex position?' I answer the question awkwardly and try to move on until a white gay man pulls the middle fingers at me and yells 'Get off the stage.' I am shaken. The yelling gets too loud for me, the lights too bright, and I am lightheaded. I might throw up. Nothing from that point on makes sense to me. My body enters an autopilot state of needing an escape. I am confused at why the judges would take us to Family Bar, knowing its reputation. The white gays who party there are notorious for racism.

The first day of the Mr Gay New Zealand competition is hellish for me. I don't sleep the night before the Big Gay Out. I am contemplating if it is worth going through with the rest of the competition. I am not going to win. All the signs are there, I just need to stop ignoring them and stop thinking I can still win if I win the most categories. I have never known myself to be a quitter. I show up to the Big Gay Out the next day in my *ei katu* (Cook Islands flower crown) given to me by a friend, my *tapa* and a Fijian *sulu* and shirt.

We are given a few hours to fundraise money for the charity component of the competition. I have noticed Elliot avoiding me all morning. Nothing awkward or rude has happened between us. I approach him because I want to understand what has happened between us. He continues avoiding me and tells me that we cannot be seen together. 'Why not?' I question him.

Elliot hesitantly alerts me that one of the other judges approached him at the Big Gay Out before I arrived that morning and asked him to reconsider the scores he gave me. Elliot gave me a 100/100 the two times he was asked to score the contestants. The other judge told Elliot that no one had received two perfect 100 scores before and gave him a chance to change his votes. Elliot did not change his scores and said the perfect 100 scores were deserved. The other judge asked him if he was sure, and when Elliot did not back down, he said 'Haha, okay, okay, perfect scores going in.'

I am doing very well in the competition, so receiving high scores makes sense to me. What does it mean that I am being scored too high? Do I not deserve the scores I am getting, or do they not want me to receive the scores that I deserve so that I won't top the categories? I am dressed up like the Queen of the fucking Nile with a sunscreen-white cast standing under the scorching hot sun in Coyle Park, fuming at this news. If it gets any hotter there'll be smoke coming out of my ears and nose. I am livid. They don't want me to win, and they are trying to do everything they can to achieve that.

The contestants are invited to the main stage of Big Gay Out to speak to the audience. This is a repeat of the night at Family Bar. A group of drunk white men standing at the front of the stage start yelling. They cheer for the two white contestants, but every time a person of colour takes the mic they yell and scream. I am anxious about speaking after the previous night.

As soon as I go to speak, one man yells, 'What have you done?'

When I speak about the need for collective action to ban conversion therapy another yells, 'That is just one thing.' I learn something unfortunate but important in this moment. The movement to ban conversion therapy is not important to many cis white gay men. Their identity has already moved into a realm of liberation, while the rest of the community is left fighting for themselves. My experiences mean little. These men appear to only have apathy for children and young people suffering in conversion therapy.

Some of the judges are on the stage with the contestants. The Big Gay Out has security at the mainstage. No one intervenes to remove the white men who are yelling abuse at the brown contestants. Yet again the brown contestants in the competition are being attacked and white queer people are refusing to use their power to stop it. The judges move on to announcing the winner of the competition. This is the moment that everyone has been waiting for. This year, Mr Gay New Zealand is the most popular that it has ever been.

I am expecting to be in the top two with Jethro. He has excelled at all of the challenges. If it's not me, I think he will be the winner. Jethro, Liam and I are left standing. Jethro is announced to be at third place. My fears are confirmed. I was sure that if I didn't win, Jethro would. I place second. The judge who had questioned Elliot comes to hug me and tells me I just missed the win because I did not raise enough money. I am puzzled by his explanation. I thought the winner of Mr Gay New Zealand is the person who wins the most categories in the competition. *Gay Express* releases the results and I have topped three out of six categories. The person who won the competition has topped two. Did the judges made a last-minute executive decision to give the title to someone who did not win the most categories?

Over those two days I learnt so much about the white queer

community. The judges were committed to finding justifications for why I shouldn't be given the title of Mr Gay New Zealand. When I topped the most categories, it seems they changed the rules of the game. I disrupted the status quo and that scared them. They weren't ready to let go of their power. In my opinion, the new Mr Gay New Zealand is not going to rock the boat. The status quo serves him as a white man. My relationship with Mr Gay New Zealand, the judges and *Gay Express* magazine, which is a key sponsor, breaks down quickly.

I need the competition to end to finally allow myself to feel and express the anger that has built up throughout it. When I get home that night, I am angry. I promise myself I won't let these people win. I divert my anger. The Cook Islands has started having a conversation about decriminalising homosexuality; however, it has backfired. The Cook Islands only criminalises homosexuality between men, but in 2020 they want to extend those laws to include lesbians as well. There is an outcry by queer Cook Islanders for support from queer people in the diaspora. I join Te Tiare Association, a queer advocacy organisation that advocates to decriminalise homosexuality in the Cook Islands, to protest the proposed law changes. Our cause is extended beyond the Cook Islands. We protest to decriminalise homosexuality in the Cook Islands, Kiribati, Papua New Guinea, Sāmoa, Tonga, Tuvalu and the Solomon Islands.

I make the hard decision to attend the Rainbow Pride Auckland parade for the protest. Rainbow Pride Auckland abandoned queer people of colour and trans people to stand in solidarity with the police. I wouldn't go to any Rainbow Auckland Pride events if I had a choice. I no longer have a choice. Pacific queer people are left in a desperate situation. We need to raise awareness about the state of the Pacific Islands urgently. The only large queer event that is

Right Me, an overweight baby at a few months old. This photo was taken about a month before Fiji's third coup, but its first ethnic coup.
© Shaneel Lal

Below My sister, Sweta, and me posing at my parent's favourite photo studio. Nearly everyone in my family had their photos taken here.
© Shaneel Lal

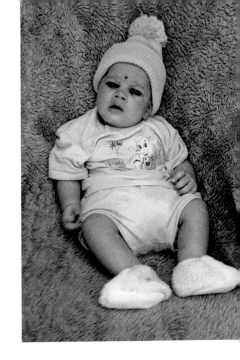

Left Ma, Pa, Sweta and me in my parent's favourite photo studio in Nausori town.
© Shaneel Lal

Below Sweta and me dressed up in saris by Pa's sister, Fua. Fua is one of the few people in my family who is accepting of who I am.
© Shaneel Lal

Left Sweta and me back in the photo studio. Sweta seems to be getting annoyed and I can't seem to keep my mouth closed.
© Shaneel Lal

Middle Me standing in one of the temples in my village. This temple holds some of my fondest moments of Fiji yet some of my most horrific experiences of conversion therapy.
© Shaneel Lal

Below Me standing in front of Pa in our kitchen in our wooden and tin house in Fiji. I still know exactly what standing in that kitchen feels like. I spent my whole childhood in this house.
© Shaneel Lal

Above My friend, Tanya and me posing in Albert Park in 2017. Tanya and I are just coming to terms with our sexualities.
© Shaneel Lal

Below I snuck out of home to go to my first pride march in 2018. It was a blast! Pictured to the left at the back in denim jeans and vest is my friend Cathrine.
© Shaneel Lal

Left In 2017, I joined the then-Minister of Education Chris Hipkins' Youth Advisory Group. I finally got to meet him in 2018.
© Shaneel Lal

Below Me in my year 13 biology class in 2018 wearing the jaw of a Homo neanderthalensis as a crown and holding the rest of the skull in my hand. My biology teacher was not happy with me.
© Shaneel Lal

Left Modelling for the Peace Foundation's website in Ōtāhuhu College in 2018.
© Shaneel Lal

Middle Smiling with my local MP Jenny Salesa moments after she chose me to be her Youth MP. This day changed my life and set me on the path to advocating for the conversion therapy ban in Parliament.
© Shaneel Lal

Below At the end of 2018, I became the Dux of Ōtāhuhu College: a dream come true.
© Shaneel Lal

Left It is 2019, and I'm speaking at Youth Parliament. This was the moment that invigorated Aotearoa to move to ban conversion therapy.
© Parliament Press Gallery

Right Posing with Labour MP Marja Lubeck after accepting my speech at the Pacific Cooperation Foundation awards in 2020.
© Shaneel Lal

Below Leading the pride march in 2021 alongside other trans activists. This year the pride march focused on transgender rights.
© Sam Sutherland for Auckland Pride

Left On my way to the 2021 pride march to protect trans rights and a ban on gay and gender conversion therapy.
© Bianca Leilua

Left With my friends Tanya, Lucy, Ammon and Amanda hanging out at Amanda's apartment in 2023.
© Shaneel Lal

Right Five years after getting involved in the movement to ban conversion therapy, I won Young New Zealander of the Year in 2023, and became the first transgender person to win an award at the New Zealander of the Year Awards since its inception in 2010.
© Tom and Nicholas Shackleton

happening is the Rainbow Auckland Pride parade, so that is where we take our cause.

Decriminalising homosexuality in the Pacific is the most pressing issue any group at the parade is fighting for. Still, the organisers of the parade place us at the back, behind the police, behind the Labour party and behind the corporates. We parade anyway. I can't not protest the police that are present at the parade as well. I go to the parade with a sign that reads, 'Your police do not make me feel safe.' Eyes roll, heads turn, and a Labour MP tells me to take the sign down. I refuse to listen.

The police are given a spot towards the front of the parade. I am at the back of the parade with Te Tiare Association. As we keep parading, an old white gay man snatches my sign and screams, 'Fuck you for ruining a lovely parade.' He is so angry that I am protesting his beloved police. He tears my sign apart. It makes me wonder, if white gays at Pride can understand homophobia as a form of oppression, then why can't they understand racism as a form of oppression in the same way? I have to move on with the parade. One cause is lost, but I still have another to keep fighting for. I have already compromised my values by attending the parade, I may as well complete the whole damn thing.

I expected the white gay men at the Pride parade to be upset by my protest sign. What irritates me is when young left-wing white gays who align themselves with Auckland Pride Festival start criticising me on social media for attending the Pride parade. The left-wing white queers shut their doors to us. They also remove us from their Friday night drag-race viewings, Saturday night parties and Sunday morning brunches. Cis white gay men, the same men who post Black squares and #BlackLivesMatter during the peak of Black Lives Matter, who present themselves as über radical and anti-racist, who call everyone they know 'e hoa', have created a culture of only-white-gay-men events, or as I like to call it, 'the e hoa generation of gays'. They aren't shy about it. They post on their Instagram very proudly that they are having a dinner, a show viewing, a party or a brunch and everyone present is white. My friends and I start playing a game called 'spot the brown person', and we usually do spot the brown person at the back, holding a tray with drinks on it to serve the white gays.

I consistently see queer and trans people of colour at the forefront of movements fighting for queer liberation. Cis white gay men do the least work but benefit the most from these movements. Ngahuia Te Awekotuku, Louisa Wall, Georgina Beyer and Carmen Rupe are all part of a brown queer history towards white gay liberation. Brown queer folk sowed the seeds and cis white gay men reap the rewards. White gay men are on TV, they are on every queer ad, they are receiving the PR packages and getting invited to the PR events. They make up a significant majority of queer organisations including Auckland Pride Festival, Rainbow Auckland Pride and New Zealand AIDS Foundation — New Zealand AIDS Foundation being the whitest. They are the spokespersons for the queer community on every single issue.

These young white gay men link themselves with Auckland Pride Festival over Rainbow Auckland Pride and see themselves as the saviours of brown queer people and trans people. I am accused of supporting militarisation of Pride and being pro-police. My relationship with the queer community is fracturing. I don't feel like I belong in this community. Maybe I never did. I most certainly don't feel like anyone has my back. I grew up trained to look out for myself, and my experiences with the queer community are reinforcing that.

18
My little
love

Blue Moon plays in the kitchen as I light a candle in Frederic's sitting room. He is tired from our dinner. So tired, he does not take his suit off. But neither do I. He looks like a true gentleman in his pearl white shirt and black blazer and pants. He is so handsome I cannot keep my hands off him. I am wearing the same. I pull Frederic off the sofa. I grab his face, and he wraps his hand around my back. The music plays softly as our feet begin to move slowly. Our feet fall in step, and we let the rhythm take control of our bodies.

I slide my hands inside his blazer and unbutton his shirt. He unbuttons mine. We throw the shirts and blazers on the couch. I move into his arms and rest my head on his chest — my head feels heavy with thoughts. I enjoy the softness of his chest. He traces the bones in my back with his fingers. We aren't in a hurry. The night is still young.

The candle provides us ambient lighting. The white walls catch a reflection of us as we slip into each other's arms. I lift my head to search for his eyes. His blue eyes glisten in candlelight, and I gently kiss him. My black locks fall over my eyes, blocking the candlelight like curtains blocking sunlight. He brushes the hair off my face and delicately tucks it behind my ear. He starts with kissing my shoulders, working his way up my neck. Our eyes lock, and we drown in each other.

The slow dance pulsates emotions through my veins, bringing back memories buried deep in my chest. I feel premature nostalgia for Fiji. My body is acting on its own. The song has changed to 'Till There Was You'. It makes me love him even more. I draw him closer when my mind snaps back to the present.

Frederic is leaving for Australia tomorrow. It is sudden. He is going to see his family and sell his house in Australia to buy a place in New Zealand. I comfort myself by thinking he will be closer to me when he returns. He asks me to keep some of his clothes while he is away. I am going to hide them in my room. We dance the night away. Our reflections on the wall flicker before disappearing when the candle burns out.

I am back at home with Ma and Pa. Not much has changed between us. We have not talked about my queerness, and I don't think we intend to anytime soon. I am in the media often. I am sure Ma has googled me and is aware of what I am up to, but she never brings it up. I don't try to hide anything from them, but I am not eager to tell them anything either. I am quiet at home because I like the peace in being left alone.

In my quiet moments, I dream of liberating queer people of colour. With Mr Gay New Zealand out of the way, I use what is left of Pride month to put pressure on the Labour party to commit to banning conversion therapy. It is Pride after all, so it is the ideal time. Politicians, even those who have voted against same-sex marriage, like Simon Bridges, show up to Pride to desperately beg for votes. Pride gives politicians an opportunity to campaign ahead of elections. 2020 is an election year, so politicians are out on the prowl for votes. They have learnt that the queer community now has an ever-growing influence on New Zealand elections. This creates the perfect climate for us to make our demands. Prime Minister Jacinda Ardern can no longer avoid two questions. The first is: why hasn't the Labour party committed to banning conversion therapy two years after Marja introduced her member's bill? And the second: if the Labour party isn't willing to commit to protecting queer lives, why are they coming to Pride and pretending to care about us?

After two years, Jacinda can no longer ignore us. She gives in and says that she is confident Marja's bill will pass if it is drawn out of the member's ballot. Marja's bill never sees the light of day. Jacinda notes that for Marja's bill to be a government bill it will need the support of the entire Government. I take away two things from her statement.

First, despite the Labour party having no party policy to ban conversion therapy, Jacinda insists that she and the Labour party support the ban. She says, 'Obviously I support it and I'm sharing Labour's position.' The Labour party is relying on Marja's member's bill, but if Marja's bill is drawn out of the ballot, the Labour party wouldn't have to support it as a caucus because they don't have a party policy supporting it. I understand Marja needed the support of the Labour party to introduce her bill to the member's ballot. A majority of Labour MPs would vote in favour of it if it were drawn, but I doubt they all would. The question remains — why is the Labour party refusing to make it a party policy to ban conversion therapy? They could still have a party policy on it whilst Marja's bill sits in the biscuit tin.

Second, the government of the day is made up of Labour, Greens and New Zealand First. In 2020, the Green party of Aotearoa New Zealand are the only political party in the Government that has a party policy supporting a ban on conversion therapy. Jacinda says Labour supports a ban, though they have no policy. This means that the only party that could be getting in the way of Marja's bill becoming a government bill is New Zealand First. Jacinda refuses to say if it is New Zealand First getting in the way. Grant Robertson states that Marja's bill doesn't have support across the Government for it to be a government bill. The fact that Labour and Greens support the ban leaves New Zealand First exposed for their apathy.

I spend a lot of behind-the-scenes time imploring Labour MPs to convince Jacinda to commit herself publicly to a ban on conversion therapy. I always get the same reply: the Labour MPs don't want to burn the Labour party's and the Prime Minister's political capital on this issue. Some Labour MPs are concerned that if Jacinda obligated herself to banning conversion therapy, it would be detrimental to them if they failed to act on it.

I would say that the Labour party is soft launching their support for queer people during Pride. Labour doesn't give us a party policy but CTAG still finds ourselves in a powerful position. We finally have the Prime Minister on record saying she supports the ban on conversion therapy. It is a political high in the movement before everything suddenly changes.

In the last week of February, the first case of Covid-19 arrives on our shores. New Zealand up till now has been a haven from Covid-19. New Zealanders have watched the harm the virus has done overseas from afar, but it is here now and no one really knows what to do about it. People are upset with politicians for not having the perfect approach to mitigating the spread of the virus, but no one does. No one in my circle has lived through a global pandemic as an adult. I am lost, confused and a little afraid, and I am praying that our first case will be our last. I think many people feel like I do. My friends and I look at each other equally confused and worried, not knowing where we are headed.

While New Zealand is facing the beginning of a raging

pandemic, Virginia becomes the first Southern US state to ban licensed medical professionals from practising conversion therapy on minors, and the Canadian Government makes a move to ban conversion therapy. Banning conversion therapy is becoming a global movement. After years of desperate attempts, we have finally got the Prime Minister to say she supports a ban and just when we do, a virus steals all the political attention. We have no opportunity to capitalise on that moment.

Frederic calls me from Australia when he isn't at home with his family. It is tricky for him to find time away from them to call me for long. Our calls are short, but I am happy to see him. I smile at him childishly, romantically, as I rest my elbow on a table, head in my hand. Sometimes we stare at each other quietly. We enjoy each other's presence.

He says, 'Promise me you will never stop dancing to our old love songs.'

'Dancing with you feels so much better, but I will continue moving to our old love songs,' I promise.

The Government begins to ramp up the precautionary measures to deal with Covid-19. On 14 March, they announce that anyone entering New Zealand must self-isolate for fourteen days, except those arriving from the Pacific. Our situation is progressively becoming dire. On 19 March the Government announces that all gatherings of more than 100 people are to be cancelled. Our borders are closed to all but New Zealand citizens and permanent residents. Frederic can't return.

Two days later the Government introduces the four-tiered Alert Level system. We stay at Alert Level 2 for two days before they move us to Alert Level 3. In 48 hours, they announce we are moving into Alert Level 4. The Government declares a State of National Emergency at 12:21 p.m. on 25 March. Mr Gay New Zealand 2020 was supposed to travel to South Africa to compete in Mr Gay World. That is cancelled, too. Oops.

In less than a week, New Zealanders go from being some of the freest people in the world to being the most restricted they've been in their lives. Outbreaks are widespread in the community. The Government tells us to stay at home in our 'bubbles'. We are required to work and study from home. Only businesses supplying necessities like groceries, petrol and medicine are allowed to remain open. We aren't allowed to travel except for necessities or to undertake safe recreational activities. Masks are mandated. No gatherings are allowed.

I am an extrovert. The lockdown is a shock to my system. They say your twenties are the best years of your life. My twenties begin with a global pandemic and a war. Could it get any worse? I am at my apartment with my Pa and Ma. Pa bickers a lot. 'Don't shower at 3 p.m.' 'Don't eat in your room.' 'Don't watch the TV at 6 p.m.' 'Take the rubbish bin out before it is dark.' He is starting to annoy me.

The world has stopped. I haven't been this still ever in my life. Lockdown starts to feel like the beginning of a *The Purge* movie. Any moment now, there could be clowns walking down my street with chainsaws, and I am so bored, I would run to them. I live next to a cemetery, but the eeriness is normally silenced by the noise of McAuley High School students playing on the netball courts. Now the students are gone, and the streets are empty of people and cars. There is a fraught silence. I have to find ways to keep myself sane.

University has shifted completely online. I am in the first year of my Law and Arts degree. It is hard enough being at Law School, but now we have to do it online. Our opportunity to interact with other students is gone. It becomes impossible to keep on track with my lectures. Being present in a room full of people doing the same thing as me allowed me to focus. While I was on campus, I was getting things done as they were happening.

Only a few days into lockdown I can't find any reason or motivation to wake up every day to watch lectures on my laptop. I get bored listening to the lecturers talk, sometimes making lectures longer than their time slot. I get exhausted from staring at my screen.

I learn something curious about my brain. I have become easily distracted and forgetful. I can't concentrate enough to complete an activity — I'll be typing a university assignment in a Word document when I need to google something. I open Chrome and there is an article already open on greyhound racing. I read the article, close Chrome and return to my Word document a few minutes later. I've completely forgotten why I opened Google in the first place. This becomes a very common experience. It takes me longer to complete my work because my ability to focus is depleted.

I start bunching up all my tasks. If you give an ordinary person ten things to do, they will likely list them and do one thing at a time until they have finished them all. I don't do that. I group all my tasks together and launch into all of them at once. I read the email for the first task, create a plan for the second, open the files for the fifth, research the eighth and ask questions about the tenth. There is no neat order to how I do things. At the end of each day, I won't have completed anything on the list. I get angry at myself for not completing my work.

When I know what I need to do, I can't start it. I'm not lazy. I know I have something to do, I want to do it, and I know there are consequences for not doing it. I somehow can't disrupt the easy and entertaining thing I am already doing and complete my work.

Even when I am doing entertaining things like watching TV I can't concentrate. I pick a TV show, watch a few minutes of it and then pick another. It isn't the ordinary loss of interest. My mind is throwing a tantrum. If I continue watching something for too long, I have outbursts of unhappy emotions. Every time I want to rest, I'm not resting. I am thinking. My mind is flooded with thoughts. These behaviours are seeping into my friendships. I can't really speak without preparing. I confuse everyone I speak to. I often forget the point of what I want to say.

I have to find a quick fix. I start making 'To Do' lists. What starts as a short bullet-point list soon becomes a very long detailed essay. I write down everything I need to do and when I need to do it. I also set alarms to tell myself to reply to an email or look at the list. I never really get to finishing everything.

The longer I stay caged in my room, the worse it gets. I don't understand what is happening with my brain. My mind is getting in the way of everything. I don't know where to turn for help. Growing up in a Pacific and Asian family means that my family don't believe in mental health or disorders and disabilities of the brain. I'd never heard the terms 'mental health' or 'wellbeing' all the years I spent in the Fijian education system, and I never saw anything about it on the TV, so my parents had no way of knowing. If I'd showed signs of anything in my childhood, my parents and teachers would never have picked it up. And if they did, there was nowhere to take me for help. The health system in Fiji was barely coping with the number of people needing dental check-ups, so I doubt they had room for 'poorly disciplined' and difficult children. My school reports always noted that I was talkative and a busybody. The attitude towards mental-health problems and brain disabilities was that those people were crazy.

I've never seen a doctor for anything other than getting vaccines at school in New Zealand. I don't have a GP and I've never properly engaged with the health system. I rarely ever get sick so there is never a need to rush me to the doctor. We know it is expensive to go to the doctor as immigrants, so we are very cautious about seeking medical assistance. I guess it would be different if we were rich but as it is, I don't go to doctors or psychiatrists for help. I wonder what life is like for people who can focus or don't have a million thoughts rushing through their heads at every given moment.

Lockdown is proving to be demanding, but I am learning a lot about myself. Frederic messages me every day, but for the last few days, I haven't heard from him. I send him many messages, and I call him many times, to no end. I am restless not hearing from him for so long. I check his Instagram and Facebook for new posts, and I search through his tagged posts. There is nothing recent. He's dropped off the internet without any notice.

I wake up on Sunday that week to a post from Frederic's sister on his Facebook timeline. I read the words 'Frederic died on Monday night, in Sydney, Australia.'

This has to be a sick prank. I cannot believe it. It just cannot be true. I rush to scroll through his Facebook and see the condolences flood in from his family and friends. Is it over just like that? How can that be? I am in disbelief.

I scroll through his Facebook only to be met with more confirmation that Frederic is gone. My breathing breaks up and my eyes well. I am in complete shock. The muscles in my face tighten, my jaw is in unbearable pain. Once the first tear breaks free, the rest rush like a storm. I cry till I am in pain. Till my stomach hurts and I am forced to fight for air. And then I cry more. My person is gone. That feeling that Frederic will never speak to me again scares every cell in in my body.

The person who grounded me, calmed me and protected my sanity is gone, and there is nothing I can do about it. I've never felt so helpless and alone. Frederic was not out to his family. Coming out was his decision, not mine. I can't throw him out of the closet after he passed away. I do not know how to approach his family. I am afraid I will out Frederic to his family by doing anything, but I need to know what happened to him.

I cannot grieve him the same way straight people can grieve the people they love. I cannot grieve publicly. I am not allowed to. Our love was hidden from the people that mattered. How do I grieve love that is prohibited? It is gut-wrenching to lose someone I hold so close to my heart. I am never going to get closure. He is gone, and I mean nothing to his family. Who do I turn to for closure and comfort?

Mourning in private is unbearable. Torturous. As unsatisfying as our end is, that is life for us. I am depressed. I lose my appetite, my passion to make the world a better place, my desire to wake up — nothing makes me feel anything. I am suffering alone. I remember my promise to him. I put on 'Blue Moon', Frederic's song. I search out his blazer hidden deep in my closet. Tears roll down my face as I hug his blazer and sway to our old love song. I wish I could bring him back.

I will never stop dancing to our old love songs.

19
He is dead, but they are here

The elections are around the corner and the political parties are throwing promises around like confetti, many of which they know they will not deliver. I tell myself to strike while the iron is hot. The Ministry of Health reports zero community cases of Covid-19, and the lockdowns are dropped. After gaining some sanity back, I am ready to agitate the Government again. But where can I turn? We have exhausted all avenues for creating public outrage at the lack of government action. We need a new catalyst for the movement. Who knew our catalyst would be the United Nations (UN)?

On 14 June 2020, the UN calls for all countries to ban conversion therapy, stating that the practice may amount to torture. UN Independent Expert on sexual orientation and gender identity Victor Madrigal-Borloz says conversion therapy practices are 'inherently discriminatory, that they are cruel, inhuman and degrading treatment, and that depending on the severity of physical or mental pain and suffering inflicted to the victim, they may amount to torture.'

This is it. This is what we need. Our activism dry spell is over.

The UN has picked up on the global trend of countries making a move to ban conversion therapy and sent a message to New Zealand that we are falling behind. Ten days after the UN calls for a ban on conversion therapy, Mexico City bans it. The Labour party takes another hit when the Greens release their election policies for queer people and emphasise their commitment to banning conversion therapy. The pressure is building on the Government from every direction when I get a call from a producer at *Breakfast*.

Breakfast wants to interview me on the topic of conversion therapy, and I say yes. I am absolutely going to do this, even though I am afraid of being on national TV for the first time in my life. I have received no media training, but I need to do this. It is a golden opportunity to enlighten and enrage New Zealanders and put out a call to action. I stay up all night preparing for the interview. I eagerly get on the train from Ōtāhuhu to Britomart at six in the morning and arrive at the TVNZ building early. While I wait for a producer to come get me, I take selfies of my reflection on a black glass wall. I am both excited and anxious. As a kid growing up in Fiji my dream job was to be a news presenter. I thought it would be so cool to present on *FBC News*. I sat in front of the TV at 6 p.m. every evening. My interest in politics started at an early age.

I am going to be on national TV, but I am going to discuss a very personal and controversial issue. No one in New Zealand knows my story of conversion therapy. I do not intend to tell anyone either. I am about to make a part of my dream as a kid come true, but I also want to do the movement justice. It is purely coincidental that I am fulfilling a tiny bit of my own dream in the process. There is a lot riding on this interview. After our long dry spell, I need to nail it. Despite the fear, I trust my abilities. I know I am the right person for the job.

The producer collects me and walks me to get my makeup and

hair done. I get my face powdered and my curly hair flattened before going to sit outside the studio. Jenny-May Clarkson runs by and calls out, 'I am interviewing you today!' Phew. I let out the breath I've been holding in all morning. I am relieved to know I am being interviewed by Jenny-May. She has a gentle touch to her interviewing.

I enter the studio. There are wires on the floor. I try not to step on or, worse, trip on them. I make my way to the couch, when I hear John Campbell shout 'Who is this bright person?' I laugh, and suddenly I am at ease. I sit myself on the couch and Jenny-May joins me.

She asks me, 'What do you think not banning conversion therapy says about us? Since your speech, Mexico City, Israel, Canada, Germany, they've all banned this kind of practice. So what does not banning it here say about us?'

I am honest. 'We have become complacent,' I respond. 'New Zealand had the Homosexual Law Reform, then the Marriage Equality Act and now we don't care enough.' My response continues:

New Zealand has successfully fabricated an international image of being a haven for queer people. When I criticise New Zealand for not doing better, I am told I should be grateful that New Zealand is not stoning queer people to death like they do in Uganda.

Why should I be grateful that the state isn't killing me for simply existing? I should not have to be grateful that the Government isn't trying to kill me. Safety is a basic human right. It's not a luxury or privilege I should be grateful for.

I know that New Zealand affords queer people more of their rights when compared to other countries, but in New Zealand young queer people are five times more likely to attempt suicide than young non-queer people. We are not doing enough.

This is not a competition for who is the most oppressed
to win the complaining rights and everyone else has to
either shut up or put up.

New Zealand is not doing enough, and it deserves to be
criticised. New Zealand has created an unshakeable image
for supporting queer rights. It no longer matters how much
or how little the Government does for queer people. The
international community has made up its mind.

Jenny-May, throwing her hands up in despair, asks, 'So what next?
Where to now?'

And I respond, 'That is the question we ask the Government.'
But what grabs New Zealanders' attention are my next few words.
Firmly, I say 'Conversion therapy is state-sanctioned torture.' New
Zealanders are shocked to hear me say that. People claim I am
sensationalising the issue. Others argue it isn't an issue at all.

My social media is flooded with support but also with the hatred
and anger of those who disagree with me. The disagreement
is primarily from extremist Christians. I told Jenny-May that 'In
the same book that says snakes can talk, it says homosexuality
is a sin, or that traditionally, marriage was between a man and a
woman. Well, traditionally, voting was between white men and the
government. Things have changed and so should we.' Oh, they are
unhappy and, apparently, unintelligent. One commentor says, 'Can
someone slap him?' Others post multiple variations of *shut up*.

I sleep the comments off. This is not my first time in the middle
of a political controversy. I received more violent messages and
comments after my speech at Youth Parliament. I have built a skin
as thick as a brick wall towards the nasty comments left on my
social media, but I am startled when I wake up to a transphobic
character-assassination piece about me in the *Manawatu*

Guardian, republished on the *New Zealand Herald's* website three days after my interview on *Breakfast*. I didn't think I was popular enough for people to attack me in mainstream media. I can control the comments left on my social media but I cannot control what people say about me in the *Herald*. My social media is a small platform, but now these attacks are published on the *Herald's* website.

Steve Elers, a senior lecturer at Massey University, wrote the column, titled 'Be yourself and be free . . . Do you', ridiculing my interview on *Breakfast*. Attached to the top of the column is a close-up of his disgruntled face. Elers' column reads:

> I couldn't stop having a good chuckle at gay-advocate and Youth MP Shaneel Lal's example of 'state-sanctioned torture' on a recent television interview.

After belittling me for my age and criticising the Youth Parliament, Elers goes on to explain conversion therapy:

> In reality, it seems that gay conversion therapy are programmes run by some Christian churches across the country who attempt to 'pray the gay away'.
> Yes, praying to stop an individual from being gay is what Lal calls 'state-sanctioned torture'.
> . . .
> No one is forcibly rounding up gay people, holding them down and making them pray.
> It is already a crime to unlawfully take away or detain someone — that's called kidnapping in Section 209 of the Crimes Act 1961.

So, if you see any Christians kidnapping gay people, please
call 111 immediately.

I stop reading. Steve Elers evidently has no idea what conversion
therapy is. I have seen for myself how conversion therapy has
destroyed the lives of people of all ages. The consequences of
going into conversion therapy don't change if the person has
supposedly 'consented' or not. Queer people never consent to
conversion therapy. We are coerced by external pressures all our
lives to change. From the day we are born, we are groomed with
heteronormativity. The colour pink is forced onto girls, and the
colour blue onto boys. I grew up in a world that made me believe
that there was something wrong with me, that I would go to Hell
for living my truth, that I would have no future, that my family would
disown me. The elders, the teachers and the priests got inside my
head and convinced me that my life would be over if I did not
change. They tried to end my life when I did not change. Mental
pressure to change was omnipresent. It hung over my head every
single day. I live this wild life. For Steve Elers, conversion therapy
is all far-removed theory. I refuse to let someone like him minimise
my trauma.

I know conversion therapy never works. We know conversion
therapy causes demonstrable harm. The Family Acceptance Project
at the State University of San Francisco found that rates of attempted
suicide by young queer people whose parents tried to change their
sexual orientation or gender identity were more than double the
rate of those whose parents did not try to change them. Suicide
attempts nearly tripled for those who experienced conversion
therapy through home-based practices by parents and intervention
efforts by therapists and religious leaders.

Then why is Steve Elers allowed to broadcast his uninformed

and harmful views to the entire country? We do not need to lead queer people into a practice that only causes harm. What we need is support for vulnerable queer people, so they don't feel like they need to change. The *Manawatu Guardian* is callous. I am protective of the queer community. I once needed protection, and I didn't get it. I wouldn't have suffered through all the pain if someone had protected me.

I continue to read the article:

> On the subject of LGBTQIA+ (yes, the letters are growing), a few weeks ago I wrote about the growing list of genders and gender pronouns.

> I pointed out that he (subject pronoun) / him (object pronoun) / his (possessive adjective) / his (possessive pronoun) / himself (reflexive pronoun) and the female equivalents have now been joined by other options, including but not limited to: ze/zir/zir/zirs/zerself; ze/hir/hir/hirs/hirself; ey/em/eir/eirs/emself; ve/ver/vis/vis/verself; ne/nem/nir/nirs/nemself; xe/xem/xyr/xyrs/xemself.

> That was not my attempt at writing in German. I noted that anyone can 'create their own pronouns' because it is apparently discriminatory to be labelled with an unwanted pronoun, so I made up my own pronoun: 'zigazig ah'. Tongue-firmly-in-cheek.

I am in disbelief at what I have just read. My head drops as I sit on my bed with my hands under my jaws, massaging my temples. There is no doubt that Steve's column means to ridicule trans people, but I keep asking myself, 'Why do they hate us so much?'

In a column that is supposedly about rebutting the points I raised in my *Breakfast* interview, Steve launches into an attack on trans people and their pronouns.

Steve ends his article with, 'I don't care what you call yourself, or whether you fancy men, women, transgenders or blow-up dolls. Be yourself and be free. Do you.'

Really? You don't care, Steve? Please, spare us the theatrics. You just wrote an article ridiculing and attacking trans people and you want me to believe that you don't care? I think you are very bothered by our existence. Steve is an angry little man, and he tried to feel powerful for once in his life by attacking a vulnerable group.

I feel the attacks on the pronouns personally. For a while now, I have been feeling trapped. I have been denying a part of myself out of fear. Being only a boy feels suffocating. It feel as though I am being held captive inside my body. I want to escape *me*. People know me as a gay man. I appreciate and value the masculine parts of me, but I adore the feminine parts of me. I love the feminine parts of me. I loved Frederic too. We kept our love behind closed doors, and it pained me. I have to stop hiding the things I love. It is time to stop hiding myself. The sooner I tell the truth, the sooner I'll be free.

I knew from a very young age that I was different, but I didn't have the language to communicate how I felt. I did not have the confidence or courage to say 'I am not a boy either'. Things are different now. I am older, I have some experience, I am confident and I can protect myself. My gender transcends language. It is a feeling of limitless joy, but it is caged by transphobia. A feeling that makes me want to fly, but the elders cut my wings before I could fly. I now have the language. I am nonbinary. I am one of *them*.

I change my pronouns from he/him to they/them. I include my pronouns in my Twitter name. My tweets are popular on Twitter and shared widely on Instagram, so my pronouns are advertised for people to know. Then come the questions about my pronouns. The most common question being, 'Are you a girl or a boy?' I am not a girl or a boy, I am the moment. I do not reply with that. I should. I avoid the questions.

Others deny the existence of nonbinary people. They say I can't use they/them pronouns for an individual person. That makes no sense to me. People use these pronouns for individuals all the time. Imagine — Aroha is at the gym, and she finds an iPhone lying around. Thinking someone's lost it, she takes the phone to the person at the counter and says, 'I think someone has forgotten *their* phone. Could you please give it to *them* when *they* come looking for it?' Aroha knows the phone's owner is an individual, but she uses gender-neutral pronouns to refer to them. People use they/them pronouns to refer to people they do not know all the time, so why won't they use gender-neutral pronouns for the people they know?

Grammar is to language what maps are to the Earth. If a river changes course, it is the map that is wrong, not the river. Language can and will continue to evolve. I am not going to spend my life being at war with my gender because some people choose to fixate on 'correct' grammar to deny the existence and validity of nonbinary people.

I am finding a way to respond to Steve's attack on trans people while opening up about my identity. My identity will undoubtedly cause a stir amongst my conservative Pacific following. They are okay with the gays, but being nonbinary will be a step too far for them. I focus on Steve's column. I make an Instagram post and put everything out there. My followers feel the same way about the column as I do. They are angry that such a vile attack on me and trans people was allowed to go ahead. I am surprised by the support from my online community.

At the same time, writer David Farrier picks up on Steve's

constant attacks on trans people. Before the hit piece about
me in the *Manawatu Guardian*, Steve wrote an utterly tiresome,
unimaginative opinion piece titled 'The bewildering politics of
gender pronouns' for *Stuff*. Steve wrote there too that 'Zigazig-ah
is my new pronoun.'

When David calls Steve out for his opinion piece in *Stuff*, Massey
University emails him that 'Massey University welcomes all staff,
students and visitors and we embrace diversity. There is no place
for discrimination or intolerance at our university or in Aotearoa
New Zealand.' David finds out that the Vice Chancellor of Massey
University has received multiple complaints about Steve's piece.
The university updates their website to say it supports diversity.
Steve remains employed and able to ridicule trans people under
the guise of free speech.

Massey University follows up with a statement to David, who
posts the reply on Webworm in his piece titled 'Homophobia,
transphobia, & Massey University'.

> Our academics routinely make public commentary as part
> of academic freedom under the Education Act. When an
> academic expresses an opinion, they do not necessarily
> reflect the position of our university.
>
> Dr Elers writes strictly in a personal capacity.
>
> At Massey we are Rainbow Tick certified and committed to
> providing a safe, respectful and inclusive environment.

Fuck your Rainbow Tick. What is the point of having a Rainbow
Tick at your university while your employee actively propagandises
against trans people? What does it mean for Massey University

to have a Rainbow Tick if they allow their senior lecturers to write and publish vile attacks on queer people and endorse conversion therapy on New Zealand's biggest media outlets? Steve's actions wholly undermine the purpose of the Rainbow Tick. The Rainbow Tick means nothing to me.

On 8 September 2020, the *New Zealand Herald* decides to stop publishing Steve. *Stuff* already let him go before Steve joined the *Manawatu Guardian*. I scream like a hyena. I have the last laugh. Oh, it makes my morning. Steve sends out a newsletter titled 'Cancel Culture Strikes Again' from his website to announce that his weekly column will no longer be published in print or on the *New Zealand Herald*'s website. What a brilliant self-own. I wouldn't announce my losses so proudly but Steve, he wants the world to know that he is a victim of the queers.

Steve is not being cancelled. He is dealing with the consequences of his own actions in attempting to cancel trans people. This is *consequence* culture. If he was willing to broadcast his views, he should have been ready to be held accountable for those views. Neither David nor I are at fault for his downfall — his own words are.

Steve adds, 'Maybe [David] fancies me or something.'

Steve's column is over, but my journey to understanding my gender is just beginning. The dilemma I face is whether I come out to my family. In Year 11, I first accepted that I was gay in public. At twenty, I am accepting that I am nonbinary. I can't come out as nonbinary without people questioning if this is just another phase. It isn't. The people who I am attracted to are the same, but my gender is not. I don't think people will understand the difference between sex, gender and sexuality. I am tired of explaining it.

I don't sit my parents or family down to explain who I am. I think I can hide behind the radical academic theory that if my sister doesn't have to come out as a woman, then why do I have to come out as nonbinary? I convince myself I am demolishing the misconception that people are cisgender by default and nonbinary by announcement. If I am being honest, I am again terrified the way I was when I was sixteen. Coming out as nonbinary to my family could mean losing them. I don't want to be vulnerable. Four years after I chose not to come out to them as gay, I still don't have the courage or compassion to extend the opportunity to my parents to understand and accept me. I don't hate myself for it, but I do feel like I wronged them.

My mind goes to what me being openly nonbinary means for the movement to ban conversion therapy. The Trans-Exclusive Radical Feminists (TERFs) and other transphobic groups are vocal about their opposition to banning gender conversion therapy. They are supportive of gay and lesbian conversion therapy being banned but they object to any protection of trans people. It makes it easier for the TERFs and the transphobes to attack our movement if a nonbinary person is at the forefront of it — and they do attack me. I am called a sexual predator and a paedophile and accused of having an agenda to sterilise all children. There is nothing they do not say about me.

My credibility as an activist suffers after people know I am non-binary. One person tweets, 'Your opinion means nothing because your pronouns are they/them.' My pronouns bear little relationship to my intelligence but there it is, transphobia discrediting all I've done, one tweet at a time. The political right argue that I have some sort of hidden agenda to make all children trans. My trans agenda is actually to ensure trans children survive and grow into happy adults. That is all I ever wanted for myself when I was a kid.

Caleb, a friend of just over a year, messages me past midnight. 'You've got to be joking me,' he writes.

I am confused by his message, so I write back, 'What do you mean?'

'You are a tranny now?' Caleb replies.

'You don't mean that, Caleb,' I write back.

'This one is on you, mate,' Caleb writes. I only truly understand the hatred for trans and nonbinary people when I lose a close friend after living as nonbinary.

I am rejected by many cis gay men in the queer community. Life is really changing for me now that people no longer see me as a gay man. I am now evil and disgusting and a threat to humanity. I think maybe it will be better for the movement if I step aside and allow someone more palatable like a cis white gay man to lead. The politicians love white gay men, the media love white gay men, and the TERFs love white gay men. White gay men love white gay men.

I stay up late at night. I turn on my table-lamp light, grab my laptop and place it on a chair, like the chair is a table. I type in the CTAG group chat, 'Hello my loves.' I call everyone my love.

> This has been on my mind for quite some time. Since living my life as nonbinary, people have been treating me differently. Some are acting like strangers. I do not understand what I have done. Being nonbinary is new to me and I do not know how to navigate the world yet. I have seen, and I have no doubt that some of you have seen comments bringing the credibility of our movement into question because of my identity. This movement is more important to me than anyone will ever understand. In light of the comments about me, and to protect our movement, I am going to leave this group. Power to you all.

I fall back on my bed without pressing send. I don't know if I want to do this. I do not know if I can sit on the sideline. I am muddled, lost in thoughts. I close my laptop and lie back down in bed. The next morning, I wake up angry. I am angry at myself for even having the thought of stepping aside. I am angry at undermining the strength and fight of trans people throughout history.

Trans people have a legacy of fighting for queer liberation. I refuse to sacrifice my true self for the sake of the movement. What is the movement worth if it comes at the cost of erasing the truth of those who fight for it? If I can't liberate myself while fighting for the liberation of my people, I am fighting a futile battle. I am sticking with the movement. The movement only gains strength from me. I can be nonbinary and a leader.

Many people congratulate me for being brave. I don't want to be brave. I want to live. I want people to stop congratulating me for being brave and to annihilate the systems that force me to be brave. I was fighting all these years to leave behind a better world. Now I am fighting to make the world a better place for me too. I have all my life ahead of me, and I don't want to spend it constantly fighting. Before I die, I want to live. I want to experience the joys and love of this world without the constraints of transphobia.

My transition burns all my bridges. I am stranded on an island of my own to swim to the end myself. I haven't learnt to swim. It is lonely to be on my own. To be nonbinary means to be in a constant state of mourning. I am mourning my friends, my family, my community, my aspirations, my safety, my freedom and my joy. I feel the least safe when I feel the most me. I have lost so much because I have accepted myself. But in all that loss, I have found myself.

As the old bridges burn, they create space for new ones. Some of my friends still love me. Some will never talk to me again. I have accepted that and moved on from those relationships. I can't change how people feel about who I am, but I can have the courage to be vulnerable and open myself to a world of possibilities.

I was waiting for the moment I would be allowed to grow up as myself. I waited for this moment all my life. It arrived bearing gifts and burdens. Although I have no years of my childhood remaining, I have all of my youth to grow up nonbinary. I wish people would understand that I am not becoming a new person. I am becoming who I always was in my most private authentic moments. If I don't live my life as that person, I won't be living at all. I was begging myself for a chance to be me. When I stop silencing that voice, there is one less person to fight and one more person who loves me.

I ache when I see young queer people with accepting comm-unities and families — everyone deserves that, but I don't have it. I was never raised under the guidance of my community or queer elders. I commit to creating that love for myself. It is difficult to love myself in a world that gives me no reason to. I commit to creating those reasons, too. I know I was born for greatness and there is nothing greater than being me.

20
Let's do this, Jacinda

Ah shit! Here we go again. Four new cases of Covid-19 are recorded in the community on 11 August 2020, moving Auckland into Alert Level 3 and the rest of New Zealand into Alert Level 2 at midday 12 August. Auckland is doing it tough. Level 3 is Level 4 but with KFC. Two days later, Prime Minister Jacinda Ardern extends the lockdown for twelve more days. It is nigh-on impossible for Auckland to get a break. As we enter our second long lockdown, Queensland over the ditch bans conversion therapy.

I don't see us coming out of lockdowns permanently anytime soon. CTAG knows we have to turn to social media. Social media activism isn't new, but it hasn't been used to carry out a movement during a lockdown to change any laws in our country. It is uncharted territory for me. I have very little skill in creating content for social media. The best I can do is plaster a tweet on a square and post it on Instagram. I start with that, and it works quite well. The only thing people are doing during the lockdowns is looking at screens: TVs, laptops and phones. Everyone is looking for something short and snappy after a full day of looking at screens, and that is what my tweets provide. They engage people easily. I know it isn't going to cut it, though. I have to employ an entirely different strategy to move everything online.

I've developed a habit of joining my Zooms wearing my boxers and a shirt throughout the lockdowns. I think everyone is doing it, but they are too shy to admit it. The one upside of lockdowns for me is that I don't have to wake up at 6 a.m., get ready and rush off to the city for 8 a.m. lectures. I save all the commute and dressing-up time. I roll out of bed, brush my teeth, do my skincare and Zoom into lectures from my bed. It is, however, an odd time to be in lockdown. The elections are creeping up and the Labour party still doesn't have a party policy to ban conversion therapy.

As part of the Royal Commission enquiry into abuse in state care, Joan Bellingham's gut-wrenching story gets the attention it deserves, a month before election day. In 1970, Joan left Cashmere High School in Christchurch to train as a community nurse at Burwood Hospital, never trying to hide that she was a lesbian. She grew up always wanting to be a nurse but when word got out that she was a lesbian, she was taken to the hospital not as a nurse but as a patient.

Joan's tutor at Burwood Hospital told her that homosexuality was wrong, and that she was depressed and messed up in her head. The tutor admitted her to the psychiatric ward of The Princess Margaret Hospital, where she was falsely diagnosed with a neurotic personality disorder. Three years after first being admitted to the hospital, she was diagnosed with schizophrenia. Over the course of twelve years, she was subjected to around 200 electroconvulsive therapies, which sent shocks through her brain with the expectation that this would cure her of her queerness.

I find Joan's story horrifying. It is like something out of *American Horror Story*. Actually, it resembles *American Horror Story: Asylum* to a T. It gives me goosebumps thinking that Joan's experience is recent history. I can understand the suffocation she felt. I feel claustrophobic thinking about what Joan went through.

I watch her interview. She says the electroconvulsive therapy destroyed her life. She lost her vision while she was receiving the shocks. Before each session she was injected with muscle relaxants that felt like razor blades going through her whole body. The headaches made her want to die. She still has scars on her head from the electrodes. She vomited and cried, asking the doctors not to do it again. Joan is over 70 years old now and she is still a lesbian, but she says she lost herself and ended up hating herself. People are who they are; conversion therapy is a bigoted attempt at bottling up parts of people that society refuses to accept.

New Zealanders get a glimpse of what I meant when I described conversion therapy as state-sanctioned torture on *Breakfast*. The country is accepting that it is a problem. This is a turning point for the movement. What began as a social media movement now captures the attention of the entire country. People are aware of the issue, and they are angry about the Government's inaction.

TVNZ's Vote Compass tool asks voters: 'Should there be an immediate ban on therapies that claim to convert someone from gay to straight?' The majority of New Zealanders want a ban: 72% of respondents supported an immediate ban on gay conversion therapy, 14% were against a ban and 12% didn't know. The poll shows an overwhelming support for a ban in New Zealand, but the problem is that this survey omits gender conversion therapy. I have no doubt the support would have plummeted if the question included gender conversion therapy. No one wants to talk about it, but I know the biggest attack on the movement is going to be targeted at trans people, and I need to brace myself for it.

It is 5 October, twelve days before election night, and the Labour party suddenly officially commits to banning conversion therapy. I feel suspicious about this sudden announcement just a few days before the election. Is the Labour party committing to a ban because they care about the queer community or because it is the best political move for their polls? Just a few months ago Labour MPs on the Justice Select Committee recommended against banning conversion therapy. Nothing has changed between the select committee report and now, so why is the Labour party changing their position? I guess what has changed is that it is time to win an election.

I treat election promises with suspicion. The Labour party could have declared their support for a ban months before the elections, but instead they waited till the middle of the 2020 election period to announce their support for a conversion therapy ban. The pressure in the media following Joan's story left the Labour party with no other option. Refusing to support a ban would tear down the Labour party's poll. The policy to ban conversion therapy becomes a leading element of Labour's 2020 election manifesto.

Minister of Justice Andrew Little posted the announcement to his Facebook page. One commenter asks, 'Why do you think this is one of the most pressing issues with NZ at the moment, don't you think priorities [should] be back on getting our economy going?' Andrew retorts: 'When is the economically ideal time to stop torturing people for existing?' Oh, snap! You go, Minister Little! Point of views change fast in New Zealand politics during the elections.

I turned twenty earlier this year. I am too young to be surrounded by such volatility all the time. I need some calm. I need to talk to a friend in the midst of all the political chaos. I have been working with Shannon on the movement to ban conversion therapy for the last year, but I don't really know him. I don't understand why he is committed to the movement. I reach out to him. It is quite late at night when I meet up with him. I sit across from him on a couch as he tells me why he joined the movement. Shannon is very soft-spoken. He is gentle and calm. I call him 'Daddy' to tease him for our age difference. Shannon is almost twenty years older than me. He doesn't mind. He knows he is pretty.

Shannon tells me a story about when he was in his twenties, a part of his life that I know nothing about. He was as young then as I am now, but he was growing up in a radically different time. It was dangerous to be queer when he was growing up, and it was harder in rural New Zealand than in the cities. In a very vulnerable moment, he says, 'Twenty years ago in the nineties in New Plymouth, Taranaki, I had a partner. We were both in the closet and we were both going to church as Christians. It eventually got to a point where he sort of sat me down and said, "I have to make a choice. I have to make a decision between a life with you as a gay man living as a gay couple or the church."'

I feel for Shannon. Shannon and I are different in age, but our stories feel alike. I sense the direction this is going in. I get nervous, hoping it is not what I am expecting. But hoping for the best does not change reality. It does not change history.

He continues his story. 'My partner decided to go with the church, and as a result he was put through conversion therapy to get the gay out of who he was. That spiralled into depression and anxiety and all sorts of problems. I knew he was damaged quite badly as a result, but I wasn't aware that he would eventually take his own life.'

Everything becomes quiet. I look at him as he stares straight ahead. He is quiet for a moment, and then he continues, 'That happened twenty years after he was subjected to conversion therapy, and that kind of shows the long-term impact of conversion therapy. It can have happened well in the past but twenty years later results in the victim taking their own life.'

I have learnt so much about Shannon's life tonight. I learnt about his youth, his love and his purpose. I feel connected with him in this moment. We have both lost someone to conversion therapy and we are both devoted to ending this cruel practice. As I learn more about him, I come to love him. Hearing him speak so candidly about his partner when he was young makes me feel I should share what happened to me in Fiji. I still have not told anyone about my own experience of conversion therapy. I fear sharing my suffering will make the movement about me.

Following Labour's commitment to the ban, the media are looking at the National party to give a position. Judith Collins, the leader of the National party during the 2020 elections, has a rather odd stance on banning conversion therapy. She and the National party won't commit to a ban despite all medical bodies calling it unethical and harmful. When she is asked what her party offers to queer people, she says, 'The same as everybody else,' which, in simple language, means nothing. Judith says that she will do more research on conversion therapy.

Te Pāti Māori declare their support for the ban. Rawiri Waititi says, 'Takatāpui are whānau.' I think that is one of the most beautiful moments of the movement. It fills me with joy to watch indigenous communities heal the wounds left from colonisation. Even though we are fighting for justice in a colonial system, we are seeing the movement heal communities.

David Seymour, leader of the ACT party, says he will not support a ban on conversion therapy.

The only party left to comment is New Zealand First. The media accuses New Zealand First leader Winston Peters of blocking the Labour party from making Marja's bill a government bill. Winston pushes back on the suggestion that New Zealand First blocked the ban on conversion therapy. 'You know what's appalling about that, what I find phenomenal is the deceit where people can't own up to their own lack of political influence and their own lack of political planning or political persuasion and have conveniently blamed New Zealand First,' he says.

Winston says the parties should be asked: 'When did you show New Zealand First your bill?' But New Zealand First was fully aware of the details of Marja's bill. It's in the members' ballot. Anyone can read it. In July 2019, I sent Jenny Marcroft, the Health and Human Rights spokesperson for the New Zealand First party, an email imploring her support for a ban on conversion therapy. In August 2019, Jenny sent me an email stating, 'New Zealand First does not currently have a policy on the banning of Gay Conversion Therapy. If Marja Lubeck's member's bill (Prohibition of Conversion Therapy) is drawn from the ballot, New Zealand First caucus will consider this legislation.'

I am not one bit surprised by this. The entire New Zealand First party voted against same-sex marriage in 2013, and a significant majority voted against same-sex civil union. The New Zealand First party has a record of voting against the rights of queer people, so it is only natural that they become a barrier to banning conversion therapy.

On the eve of election day, I put on my mesh top under my leopard body suit and throw on denim jeans to give a country edge. I go to GAY with Neihana Waitai. Political parties are prohibited from campaigning on election day. Neihana and I cannot do anything at this point to change the results of the election. Neither of us have led a campaign of this size before. We are both learning many of our skills on the job, so to speak. Tonight, we are going to be as carefree as possible. We are both young, queer and indigenous to the Pacific. Our joy is rare but revolutionary. We are going to forget about the tumultuous ride to this point and the long journey ahead of us, just for tonight. It is necessary to find pockets of joy to sustain ourselves. The DJ plays *Starships* and, honey, Neihana and I hit the dance floor. I am doing Cirque du Soleil, nailing my jump splits and high kicks. We dance the night away.

Election day is finally here. I spend the morning with my friends Latayvia Tualasea-Tautai and Priyana Vijay in a park near Ōtāhuhu College. The Labour party is polling higher than any party ever has. I think they are going to break the MMP system tonight. If they win, they will ban conversion therapy. I am excited and nervous. I feel differently from last night. The reality has settled in. Everything is riding on this election. If Labour wins, we will get the ban. If Labour does not, National and ACT will never allow a ban to become law. A three-year delay for the ban will be disastrous. I have not cared about or understood any of the previous elections. I know they happen every few years and we had a change in government last election, but I didn't really understand the importance of that. Now I do. I want Labour to win but I don't want a Labour-only government. A one-party government is never a good idea. They have no checks and balances.

I slick my hair back and put on a black turtleneck and my big diamond earrings. I march through Auckland CBD to Labour candidate for Auckland Central Helen White's office to meet Neihana again, this time in a more serious, less gay setting. It is comforting to be with someone who is fighting the same fight and hoping for the same results. Neihana is hopelessly devoted to the Labour party. I support the Greens and Te Pāti Māori at this election. But Neihana and I want the same thing — the best for our community, and we know the way to get that is through a Labour and Greens government. As the night goes on the election results start rolling in and the cheers in Helen's office begin. Labour is leading from the outset.

'What time is it now?' Neihana asks me.

'It's 6:48,' I reply. I have butterflies in my stomach.

'So, in about twelve minutes the results will start coming out,' Neihana says.

Anxiously I reply, 'I'm too nervous to sit.'

The two of us are glued to the news. I am leaning on a chair watching the television screen as Patrick Gower reports, 'Tonight we will have votes counted early and in big numbers.'

'The Greens are polling very well,' Jessica Mutch McKay adds.

I look at Neihana while holding his hand tightly and say, 'More than two years of work to ban conversion therapy — this is it.'

He repeats, 'This is it.'

Patrick's commentary overpowers the sound of my voice, but what he is saying is music to our ears — 'All over the country National MPs are losing their seats.' I lean further into the chair and rest my chin on my hand. At this point, if I lean in any further, I will simply collapse.

'It all comes down to this. So, with 50.2% and I am actually going to go out on a limb here, guys, and call it for Labour. I think they're going to win,' Patrick says.

The room erupts in applause and Neihana screams, 'YES!' There is no doubt the Labour party is going to win this election. Now it is just a matter of who is going to be in government with them.

We need Labour, Greens and Te Pāti Māori to win 61 seats to ban conversion therapy. Labour win 65. They don't need any other political party to form a government or ban conversion therapy. This has never been done under MMP. Jacinda becomes the most successful prime minister under MMP. Greens win ten seats and Te Pāti Māori wins two. Together, Labour, Greens and Te Pāti Māori have 77 seats. A gay that does maths? Rare but we exist. We are set to ban conversion therapy. We are unstoppable now.

21
'GO TO HELL HOMO'

I am woken by the sound of thunder. I thought it was my alarm. I pick up my phone to check the time. The bright screen light irritates my eyes. It is only 4 a.m. I do not have to get up till eight. I hear the thunder crack again. I sit up, open my curtain a little and see the lightning colour the tar-black sky white. Soon it fills my room with light like someone has turned on the switch. It is looking like a gloomy morning. I crawl back under my blanket and fall asleep.

I am awake again at two sharp bangs. It must be thunder. It's 6 a.m. and I am cranky. I turn over and go back to sleep. *Bang bang*. It's Ma — she is persistent. I finally give in and wake up. Ma holds a note in her hand, a white scrunched note that says, 'GO TO HELL HOMO' in red ink. She found it taped to our front door as she was leaving for work. I am still incoherent, not really understanding what is going on. Ma has a sense of urgency, and I need to do something quickly, but I have no clue what that something is. I wipe the sleep out of my eyes.

I don't trust the police, and there is no way I am going to call them at dawn. The police left the Pride march in protest when queer people of colour said the police made them unsafe. Their actions consistently show me they aren't interested in protecting people of colour. Why would I call them? With what hope? I have spent years in New Zealand watching videos of the police abuse their power to hurt brown children. Lying in bed, I do not think I have any safety options. I am receiving this note after a week of being attacked on Twitter by a right-wing political party. My address must have been leaked.

After the numbness from the shock wears off, I get angry. That note didn't come out of the blue. After my speech at Youth Parliament I became an easy target of the political right. I am constantly receiving threatening messages on social media. My number was leaked after my media interviews earlier this year. I have been getting calls telling me to go to Hell.

Every time I try to start a conversation about anti-queerness, people shut it down with their same old stories about how queer people in New Zealand have it so much better than those in the Middle East. But we do not live in the Middle East. We cannot control the laws of the Middle East. We live in New Zealand, and we have direct control over our culture. People whinge and moan about all sorts of things, roads, cycleways, public transport, hospitals, but no one tells them to shut up and put up with it because the roads in New Zealand are better than those in a third-world country. Instead, people get angry at the government for failing to uphold the safety of road users. Why then do we tell queer people to be grateful for crumbs in New Zealand because another country doesn't afford queer people any rights? Poor treatment of queer people in New Zealand isn't justified by the murder of queer people around the world. Hatred will never be justified.

We have spent too many years pretending we don't have a problem of anti-queerness, but denial of that problem is worse in New Zealand than it is in the brown and Black majority countries New Zealanders point fingers at. New Zealand still allows the torture of queer people under the guise of conversion therapy. Is this not bad enough?

Young queer people are five times more likely to attempt suicide than young non-queer people. Still not bad enough? When is it bad enough for queer people in New Zealand to have the right to 'complain'? Do New Zealanders want the government to chase the queers in battle tanks for it to be considered bad enough? I am angry that I was sent this hate and I am angry that there is nothing I can do about it.

Towards the end of 2020, I receive an email telling me I am being given an award for leadership from the Pacific Cooperation Foundation. The award ceremony is held at the Beehive in Wellington. In the audience are politicians including Aupito William Sio and Judith Collins. Aupito voted against same-sex marriage in 2013, but being a member of the Labour party and the Government means that he has no choice but to vote in favour of the Labour party's bill to ban conversion therapy.

I wear a blue satin shirt and black pants, with drop diamond earrings and my hair down. I attend the ceremony with a co-activist, a co-conspirer, who is also receiving an award on the night, Aigagalefili Fepulea'i Tapua'i. Fili understands my experiences as a young brown activist in politics, because she has lived them too. I have written a polite acceptance speech. I am speaking to a Pacific audience, and I don't know what to expect — they might turn out to be conservative. When my name is called, something changes in me. I don't want to maintain decorum for the sake of maintaining decorum. There are powerful Pacific people in the room, and they need to hear the reality of queer Pacific people.

I walk to the podium, accept my award, and decide to change my speech. For a long time, I have been afraid of being vulnerable with my people because I fear their rejection. Tonight, I choose to be honest. The fear of rejection is there. I acknowledge it and put it to the back of my head. This speech will take courage, but it has to be done. I start:

I was born in Fiji and Fijians are known to be some of the kindest people. But that kindness comes with an exception. Two years ago, on the International Day Against Transphobia, the body of a trans woman was found lying in a pool of blood in the capital of Fiji. A year before that, a gay couple was attacked and left to bleed. I was afraid of growing up in Fiji.

When I moved to Aotearoa, I escaped a country that was ready to kill me and a government ready to justify it. But people close to my heart at home don't have the luxury to be who they are in safety. My people in Tonga, Sāmoa, Cook Islands are considered criminals. I cannot be free until all my people are free.

In this endless cycle of homophobia and transphobia there is only one winner: the coloniser. The white gays in the Pacific abandoned the fight for queer liberation after getting gay marriage. But indigenous queer people have been left to fight our battles ever since we were colonised and criminalised. If we, as Pacific people, uphold colonial systems of bigotry, a day will come when we will cease to exist. And that day, the dreams of our ancestors will be crushed.

Every time I speak to Pacific people about the pain of queer people, there is a voice in my head that says no one is listening and no one is caring. But tonight, I hope that voice is wrong.

The temperament of the room becomes serious. Some in the audience look uncomfortable, awkwardly looking around to seek consolidation from others. Did I go too far? When you get up on a stage and start speaking you can tell by the look on people's faces if you are crashing. But there are people like Fili in the audience, rooting for me, so I continue:

I get told that the younger generation is getting weirder. That's not true. There aren't many old people like me because they are dead. Maybe it was the AIDS pandemic or making homosexuality punishable by death or the hate crimes against our community or conversion therapy. There is a generation of queer people who are growing up making dangerous mistakes because our role models were killed by the negligence of the state.

My community dies every day, and I am tired of putting up with it. I don't want your approval and I am not going to beg for it. I demand my rights. I am human as is every other queer person, so find it in yourself to let us live. Our stories are about suffering. But our ancestors were able to laugh in the face of the coloniser while enduring the pain of colonisation. Queer people have inherited that fight .

Brian Tamaki said we caused the earthquakes in Christchurch and Israel Folau said we set Australia on fire.

We have hit the ground running.

> As a kid, I was made to feel that there was something
> wrong with me. But I have learnt that there is nothing
> wrong with who I am, but there are a lot of things wrong
> with this world. We are powerful because we have survived.
> I am queer, I always have been, and I always will be. It is up
> to you to choose whether you will be a coloniser or
> an ancestor.

I leave my people with that challenge — will you be a coloniser or an ancestor?

I choose to give my people an opportunity to show me they care. I have never been brave enough to allow my parents this opportunity. It feels easier this time. The cornerstone of indigenous queer experience is that it is infused with trauma, a desire for healing and a yearning for connection to our people. I have been holding on to so much anger and resentment towards my people for the harm they've caused queer folk, but I have to accept that there are some apologies I am never going to get. Holding on to all this anger and resentment is only hurting me. The thing about having to forgive people who never apologise is that you have to watch them move on with their lives while you have to deal with all the trauma they caused you. It is up to Pacific peoples if they want to live by their own culture or by the colonisers'. Holding on to their hatred only makes it harder to heal. I let it go tonight.

I forgive them for me.

22
Lonely

I am 21 — reaching this age is a special time for all young people. I've always appreciated being born in January 2000. I never forget my age or have to do complicated maths. Covid-19 and the lockdowns have disrupted my entry into my twenties, but now that we haven't been in a lockdown for three months things are looking up. I am in my peak youth, and I am looking forward to an incredible year of partying and sex, in other words just doing what other young people are doing. I tell myself I will start gymming and learn how to drive. I intend to get my life in order and keep it together.

With their landslide victory Labour has absolute control of what the bill to ban conversion therapy will look like and when it will become law. They begin procrastinating. They say the bill will not be introduced into Parliament until the end of 2021, and it will come into effect at the end of 2022. Well, there goes the time for partying and sex. Political apathy is the bane of my youth. The time leading up to the elections was the trailer; now we are about to get the full picture.

I am already frustrated that after the elections the MP holding the ministerial profile for justice has changed. CTAG has worked with Andrew Little for the last two years to bring him up to speed with the issue. Andrew knows me so well; he once sent me an email titled, 'Shaneel and followers', as a response to the queer community asking for a ban on conversion therapy like I was the ambassador for the gays. Now the Minister of Justice is Kris Faafoi. There are no issues with Kris, but we know we have to go through the entire process again.

CTAG and I, and other grassroots activists, are unhappy with such an unnecessary and prolonged delay. The Labour party doesn't have to start from scratch. They have Marja's bill to work from and the bills of other countries who have beaten New Zealand to ban conversion therapy. I refuse to accept their timeline. I am not having it. This timeline is wrong, and it needs to change. The Labour party made the conversion therapy ban a central part of their 2020 election campaign, but after winning the election, the issue doesn't feature in the first year, let alone the first 100 days. We are being let down by the Labour party again.

What do I do? For most New Zealanders it is enough that the Labour party has committed to the ban in their election campaign. Their anger is gone. The lack of anger is more frightening to me than the Labour party's delay. The Labour party can do whatever it wants now, and a majority of New Zealanders will be at ease with it. I cannot do anything to create enough pressure on the Labour party to act quicker, but I also cannot allow this feeling of helplessness to get in the way of trying. How do I convince people that they need to get angry again?

I need to tell people that we have an issue, I need to instil a small amount of fear about the reality, and I need to give them something they can do about it. I launch an online campaign called 'Write for Human Rights'. It is a campaign to write letters to the new Minister of Justice urging him to make a move to ban conversion therapy. The uptake of writing is slow, and I start doubting myself. Have I lost my ability to rally people around a cause? Have people stopped caring about what I have to say? I think I should remove the campaign entirely, pretend it never happened and make an excuse if someone asks about it. But if I do that, then I will never know if this would have taken off later in the month. I allow it to stay on Instagram, hoping for the best but not expecting anything.

I wake up one morning to one of my Instagram followers printing the letter out and hand-delivering it to the Minister of Health's electorate office. Iconic. More people post about delivering the letters. Hundreds of people start writing emails to Kris Faafoi. Many people voted for the Labour party because they campaigned so strongly on upholding queer rights. People are rightfully pissed, and I am channelling their anger into action.

My Write for Human Rights campaign brings the attention back to the issue, and now all politicians are under the microscope. Judith Collins, having been thrashed at the election, is looking for redemption. But I think no one told Judith what she should have been doing if she wanted to be liked by New Zealanders. During the 2020 elections, Judith said she needed to do more research on banning conversion therapy before she could take a position on it. It was unclear from the get-go what she needed to research. You'd need to be living under a rock to not know what conversion therapy is. Or in Judith's case, an ivory tower. Months have passed since the election debate, so we assume she must have done the research she promised to do.

Newshub interviews her and asks, 'During the election campaign you said you would do some research on conversion therapy. Have you done that research?'

'No, I have not,' Judith replies.

'Does the National party then have a position on conversion therapy?'

'No, we have not,' she responds.

No position is a position. Judith is choosing to be complicit in the abuse and suffering of queer people. I am not surprised that the National party is picking an anti-queer stance.

A majority of the National party voted against the Homosexual Law Reform and Marriage Equality acts, and a majority of them voted in favour of defining marriage as only between a man and a woman. Todd Muller, Judith's predecessor, said he wasn't interested in the representation of queer MPs in the National party. Simon Bridges, Todd Muller's predecessor, voted against marriage equality and had previously said that he was 'not really into homosexuality'. Gerry Brownlee, the deputy leader of the National party under Judith's leadership, said in his speech against same-sex civil union that 'Homosexuals are now saying they want to be treated the same as other people. In my view, the sad fact is — although some find this difficult to take — they are not the same.'

Queer people do not have the luxury of neutrality. Judith is the leader of the opposition and as such she is responsible for holding the government to account, but she has no interest in supporting queer people.

I tweet my frustration and Twitter flea National MP Chris Bishop replies to my tweet saying that 'Bills get discussed by caucus before decisions are made. As far as I can see there isn't a Bill? Or even a timeline for one?'

'The leader of your party has confirmed the National party has no position on banning conversion therapy. Maybe your leader has been making decisions without your input, Chris,' I retort.

'Gidday, drop me an email re your offer if you want to chat on the issue. I'm a member of the cross-party Rainbow group so semi-familiar with the issues,' Chris tweets back at me.

I take him up on that offer. I email his office and schedule a time to meet him. Chris is in Auckland for a meeting at the University of Auckland. Max and I meet Chris after his meeting in the evening at the university cafe, Shaky Isles. He admits that Judith's comments were foolish. Chris tells me that he wants me to know he is an ally to queer people in the National party. He says I can trust him. Albeit with scepticism, I believe him.

Just as I think the anger at the Labour party's inaction is dissipating, Ms Judith *Talofa* Collins' comments reignite the flames. New Zealanders are furious again, and our campaign gives them something to do about it. Judith's comment makes Labour's inaction even more aggravating to New Zealanders. We tirelessly lobby the Labour party. This is the most public pressure the Labour party has had since the elections. If we can't persuade them now, we can't do it ever.

Unexpectedly one morning, I receive a call from a Labour backbencher. Her message is music to my ears. She says the Labour party has reflected on their timeline to ban conversion therapy and has decided to change it. She gives me the new timeline to ban conversion therapy. I try not to squeal with delight. Our Write for Human Rights campaign worked!

The bill to ban conversion therapy will now be introduced in the middle of 2021 with the ban being implemented in February 2022 at the latest. The ban has been brought forward by six months. I am dancing with glee on the phone. This is confidential information. I can't tell anyone about the changes yet. The new timeline is set to be announced by the Prime Minister at the 2021 Big Gay Out on 14 February. I am overwhelmed with excitement, but I have to sit on this secret for just a few more days.

A week later, Judith Collins googles conversion therapy and decides that she supports a ban.

The Big Gay Out is here. I can't control myself. I am getting jitters. I am so nervous that if I eat something, I will throw it up immediately, which is ideal because I am obsessed with being skinny. I am wearing blue high-waisted pants and a golden metal crop top. My stomach is exposed, and I feel ugly if I do not look very thin. My golden hoops rest on my shoulders. I do not drink any water or eat anything in the morning to avoid bloating. 'The thinner, the better,' I tell myself.

I sit myself down on my bed and process the importance of today's announcement. I am working as a researcher for a TV show, *Queer and Here*. I need to arrive at the Big Gay Out early to make sure people are at the right place at the right time to be recorded for the show. Then I realise that I have to take public transport from Ōtāhuhu to Coyle Park. There is no way I can travel safely, harassment-free and with my good mood and bussy intact in this outfit on public transport. I pop my earrings off and take off my crop top. I put on a casual shirt and pack the crop top and hoops in a bag.

I catch my second bus in Point Chevalier. As I get on the bus, a group of teenagers at the back of the bus start cheering and clapping loudly. They are all dressed up in glitter and rainbow capes. I know they are queer. I think the clapping and cheering is for me. The bus stops at the next stop for other people headed to the Big Gay Out and the young people start cheering and clapping again. Then I realise these queers are cheering for all the queers.

I arrive at Coyle Park bright-eyed and bushy-tailed. I run to the *Queer and Here* team and the show lead, Aniwa Whaiapu, helps me put on my crop top and golden hoops. I am shining like a disco ball. If the DJ pumps the beat, I'll be runway ready. Honey, the gays are loving every moment of it, and I am fawning.

The Green party launches a petition at the Big Gay Out demanding that the Government ban conversion therapy. I know the timeline to ban conversion therapy has already changed. I cannot tell the Greens to stop petitioning to ban conversion therapy. I cannot oppose it either. We need a united front. The

Conversion Therapy Action Group becomes one of the key drivers of the Greens' petition.

I am eagerly waiting for Prime Minister Jacinda Ardern to announce the new timeline to the public, when a siren sounds off on my phone. I think any minute now the Purge will start, and I will hear the words 'Commencing at the siren, any and all crime, including murder, will be legal for twelve continuous hours. Police, fire and emergency medical services will be unavailable until tomorrow morning at 7 a.m. when the Purge concludes. Blessed be our New Founding Fathers and New Zealand, a nation reborn. May God be with you all.'

It is not the beginning of the Purge. I look at the news headlines — 'Three new cases of Covid-19 recorded in the community. Auckland moves to Alert Level 3 at 11:59 p.m.' Not this. Covid-19 is giving homophobic. It is giving 'I hate the gays'. And I want to throw hands with it. I am not angry or upset, I am annoyed.

All the Green MPs leave Coyle Park immediately. The Labour MPs who are already at the Big Gay Out stay behind. Jacinda is yet to arrive. I rush to Marja and Shanan Halbert. They will know if Jacinda is still coming. Marja tells me she isn't. Jacinda is heading back to Wellington to announce and prepare for the lockdown of Auckland. Jacinda is no longer available to announce the new timeline.

Five days later, Auckland moves down to Alert Level 1. On 22 February, Minister of Justice Kris Faafoi steals the Prime Minister's thunder with the announcement of the new timeline to ban conversion therapy. In his press release titled 'Government reaffirms urgent commitment to ban harmful conversion practices', Minister Faafoi says, 'The Government has work underway to develop policy, which will bring legislation to Parliament by the middle of this year with the aim of having a ban passed into law by the end of this year,

195

or by February 2022 — at the latest.'

The power of the people wins again. It is a gift to be able to experience the power of being a grassroots activist. Grassroots activists and survivors are doing the most influential work in the movement. To be one of those people is one of the greatest blessings. We are living our history. We are creating our history. We are in control of our history.

The Ministry of Justice starts a community consultation — a consultation that I am intentionally kept out of. The Ministry does not mention to me that they are going to queer people, especially survivors and victims of conversion therapy, to ask them how conversion therapy should be banned. I fear the Labour party is avoiding me. I start getting messages from queer folk asking me if I have been a part of this process. The Labour party's commitment to the ban is questionable from the beginning. I think the Ministry of Justice is avoiding me so they can put forward a bill that I will be unhappy with.

I feel like they want to ostracise me from the movement. Some Labour MPs want to credit Young Labour and Rainbow Labour for the entirety of the movement. Labour knows that Rainbow Labour will not question the quality of the Labour party's bill. There are white queer people in the Labour party who are writing comments on Facebook that I am unfit to lead the movement. Some come to conversion therapy Q&A panels and question why I am leading the movement. The most vicious comment is that I do not understand conversion therapy. People repeatedly undermine my knowledge and skills and minimise my experiences. As aggravating as that is, retorting would only add fuel to their fire. I keep quiet and keep doing the work.

I cannot deny this unwavering feeling of loneliness. I constantly feel like people do not want me to be a part of the movement.

There are many people who want to stake a leadership claim in the movement to ban conversion therapy, but there are very few ready to do the work it takes to lead this mammoth. It requires skill, and strategy, commitment and perseverance. Leading the movement has more boring moments than grandstanding media moments. Many think that if they are the face of the movement, they will become popular. That is the worst reason to get involved in any movement.

I am already alone coming into politics as a young brown immigrant. I have few connections. I didn't grow up with these people, and it is impossible to break into the queer cliques. I was even more alienated when I entered queer activism. I don't know what to do. Should I quit? I have never felt this weak in the movement before. It is depressing to know that there are people working to remove me. I feel like I don't belong here anymore. I am so gravely alone, but I cannot let these white gays kick me to the side. I am not a pushover.

The Greens invite me to table their petition in Parliament on 23 February. In 1985, the Coalition of Concerned Citizens presented a petition opposing the Homosexual Law Reform Bill on the steps of Parliament. The organisers claimed the petition received more than 800,000 signatures. They brought petition sheets in 91 boxes. The Coalition of Concerned Citizens argued that decriminalising homosexuality would lead to a moral decline and the spread of AIDS. Labour MP Geoff Braybrooke and National MPs Graeme Lee and Norman Jones, who all staunchly demanded that Parliament not legalise 'sodomy', were present at the steps of Parliament to accept the petition. Parliament's Petitions Committee rejected the petition because many petition sheets contained several signatures in the same hand, and some of the boxes were nearly empty.

One Of Them

The Greens' petition receives over 150,000 signatures, making it the most signed petition to ever be tabled in Parliament. All those years ago, those bigots stood on these very steps and fought against my humanity. Today, I am standing here to fight back. I am taking my power back. The voices and actions of the white gays who tried to remove me from the fight to end conversion therapy are nothing compared with the power I feel in this moment. Although it is difficult to feel it on most days, I belong here.

I am destined to be here.

23

'No LGB without the T'

I arrive at Albert Park with my friends Brianna and Cherelle Fruean and Bianca Leilua for the 2021 Pride march. I bring the *ngatu* Siteri's mum gifted me. Brianna, Cherelle and Bianca wrap it around me on Princess Street. The *ngatu* is still long, brown and beautiful, but it is weak. It no longer has the strength to stand upright when wrapped around me. After wrapping the *ngatu*, we join the people assembled outside the bandstand in Albert Park.

I have a double-sided sign. One side of the sign says 'TRANS POWER, BIPOC POWER, QUEER POWER, PACIFIC POWER, YOUTH POWER, ALL THE POWER TO THE PEOPLE'.

The other side of the sign says 'LOVE DOESN'T NEED A CURE. END RELIGIOUS CONVERSION THERAPY'.

I am surprised by the number of Pacific people present at this year's Pride march. It is the most diverse a Pride event has ever been. Then I hear the cackling of the Ballroom community and it clicks — the Pride march this year is being led by three Pacific trans women who pioneered the Ballroom Scene in Aotearoa.

The underground Ballroom Scene emerged in New York City in the late twentieth century. It was created by Black and Latino trans and queer Americans in protest against the racism and queerphobia they faced from the non-queer community and the white queer community. The Ballroom Scene created multitudes of categories that people walk. By walk I mean compete. The categories include runways for 'femme queen realness', 'butch queen realness', 'voguing', 'face', 'sex siren' and 'body'. Femme queen realness is for trans women only, and realness is a reference to a trans woman's ability to pass for a cisgender woman. Butch queen realness is normally for cisgender gay men. They are judged on their ability to pass for heterosexual.

If people decide to walk the runway, they better come correct or they will feel the burn of a chop. That means get your raggedy ass off the runway. People mostly walk in houses. Houses function as families. Houses are led by mothers and fathers who are experienced members of the Ballroom community. The rest are 'children' of the house.

The mothers of the House of Coven-Aucoin, the House of Iman and Fale Aitu are leading Pride March 2021. The Ballroom community is out in droves to support the trans women of colour leading the march.

I stand beside the hut as the house mothers speak to the history of queer liberation and the importance of protecting trans people of colour. From where I am standing, I see a man wearing a potato sack floating through the crowd with a Bible. A moment later I see more people moving through the crowd with Bibles and pamphlets. I cannot figure out what the pamphlets say, but I sense the Bible-thumpers have arrived to rain on our parade. A rage ignites in me. I don't have enough time to think before the march begins and everyone starts walking.

We march from Albert Park to Aotea Square chanting, 'Trans lives matter.' The people on the mics repeat, 'What do we want?' and we reply, 'Trans rights!'

'When do we want it?' they shout.

'Now!' we chant.

Last year's march was underwhelming. Anticlimactic even. It was a group of people walking from point A to point B without any purpose. This year is different. As a community, well, at least those who are here, we have found a common goal.

I am walking in the march, clicking my fingers in rhythm with the chant, feeling my fantasy when I hear the word 'repent'. I was right, these are Bible-thumpers, and they are following us to Aotea Square. I take a deep breath in and roll my eyes but keep marching. I push my sign further towards the sky. When we arrive at Aotea Square, the crowd disperses to enjoy the Pride party. The religious group that was following us splits up and starts walking through the crowd yelling 'Repent' and 'God hates sin'.

I am livid. I am about to burst into flames. I tell myself I am not going to cause a scene. It is a beautiful day and the 'Christians' are here to ruin it. That is what they do best — they take beautiful things and people and destroy them. It happens every single year. Religious extremists show up with their Bibles to Pride to call queerness a 'sin' and queer people 'sinners'. I've had enough of it.

Why did their church send a troop of God's fan club to Pride march to preach that God hates sin? Their services are neither paid for nor required. If I want the church in my pants, or my life, I will fuck a father. I don't care what their Bible told them. I will support Christians to live a life free from persecution for what they believe in, but I will not tolerate Christians imposing their beliefs on others. A book about a mythical man in the sky will not dictate how I live my life. It will most certainly not extinguish my rights.

Despite the Christian extremists tussling though the crowd for over an hour, I don't say anything. As my friends and I are leaving Aotea Square, a girl claiming to be a messenger of the Messiah walks over to my friend Latayvia to hand her a pamphlet. Latayvia waves no and refuses to take it. I am disgusted by that girl's audacity to come up to my friends.

Enough! Queer people never show up to Christmas service, or an Easter event at church and yell 'Repent' and 'God hates sin' at Christians. You don't see me lip-syncing to 'Raining Men' outside church every Sunday. If queer people did that the church would cry persecution. Christian extremists have consistently terrorised queer people in the name of God, and they have got away with it each time. Not today, Satan. Not today. Our battle of words ensues as the music blasts on the big speakers near the stage.

Me: Why are you here?

Messenger of Messiah: What is your perspective on how [your family] view religion or how they believe in Jesus Christ?

Me: They believe in equality and love for all. The God you speak of is not a God that hates, it's a God that loves everyone regardless of who they are.

Messenger of Messiah: But he hates sin.

Me: What is the sin, darling? What is the sin?

Messenger of Messiah: Sin is breaking a commandment—

Me: No, no, what is the sin that I am committing here?

Messenger of Messiah, stuttering: The sin, I never pointed out anything, you can decipher it yourself.

Me: Let me ask you. Why are you at a Pride march telling me that you hate sin, and God hates sin. Who are you? Who are you to tell me that God hates sin at a Pride march?

Messenger of Messiah: A messenger of the Messiah.

Me: This is supposed to be the space of queer people. This is not supposed to be a space where religious people

come and preach bigotry. We have been persecuted
by the church for years and years and we are sick of
putting up with it.

Messenger of Messiah: Yup.

Me: Do you realise that there are young people here that
will be harmed by you, that will consider suicide and will
be pushed to depression because of what you do?

Messenger of Messiah: What am I doing?

Me: Exactly, question yourself. What are you doing?
You're embarrassing yourself. We as a community are
sick and tired of putting up with you, so we are not
putting up with anymore.

Messenger of Messiah: You are obviously very triggered by
me just being here.

She is smirking at me at this point. It takes everything in me to not slap the smirk off her face. This is what religious bigots do. They rile up their victims and stand there smirking as their victims retaliate and get painted as the intolerant party. Anyone who speaks out against the church is villainised. It is the church that is causing harm. I didn't build my closet. Non-queer people built the walls around me, locked me inside and threw the keys away. Enough. Not one more person will be pushed in the closet because of Christian bigotry. Not one more vulnerable life can be lost in the name of Jesus. I don't care what I look like in this moment. There is no strategy at play from my end. I am raging. She thinks she is so smart for what she is doing.

She came for a sermon. I am going to give it to her.

Me: There is a fine line between religious freedom and
religious bigotry. You, telling me that God hates sin at a

Pride march is religious bigotry. You know what religious people have been able to do? They've been able to take our relationship with faith and God and weaponise it against our community and manipulate us into thinking that God will hate us if we don't repent. That is bullshit. God doesn't care if you are gay or trans, being a decent human will suffice. As for religious people like you, you have pushed queer people into a life of pain, misery, death, and God will never forgive you for that.

The church members are standing behind the Messenger of Messiah, and the queer community behind me. The church is not going to walk onto our turf and tell us that we are wrong for existing. That we are wrong for loving. I am over it. Officially. Don't like gay sex? Don't have it. Don't like gay marriage? Don't have it. Don't like queer TV shows? Don't watch them. Don't like a Pride march? Don't attend. Perhaps Christian extremists should consider turning a blind eye to queer people like they turn a blind eye to homeless children.

I look around to see if we can get help. Young queer people are being forced to listen to this anti-queer garbage. I don't want them to hear any of this hatred and internalise it. Nothing these self-proclaimed messengers of the Messiah are saying is correct. I notice the police standing and watching us as the religious group continues yelling at queer people. I walk up to them and say, 'Do something,' and the policeman sneers back at me with, 'We are busy.' Busy with what? Standing?

What are they waiting for? Are they waiting for me to get hit before they intervene? The last two years flash before my eyes. White gay men abandoned vulnerable people in their community to side with the police. This is the police that the white gays left

Auckland Pride Festival for, the police who are working overtime to excuse themselves from protecting queer people. When are the white gay men going to accept this?

The police tell the media a different story.

In a statement to the *New Zealand Herald*, police say that no laws were broken.

> 'Police are aware there was a group preaching religious beliefs near the Pride party at Aotea Square on Saturday night,' the spokesperson said.
>
> Our role was to monitor the overall event in the public space, to ensure the safety of all and respond to any issues that may arise.
>
> In general, under law police need to be mindful around the rights of all parties around freedom of expression in a public place. On this occasion police were present and were monitoring the situation. There was no unlawful activity identified.

Christian fundamentalists are in bed with the state, and the police have no interest in protecting queer people. The police are telling us something important. In their view, yelling, 'God hates sin' and 'Repent' at queer people at a Pride event is merely 'preaching religious beliefs' and an exercise of 'freedom of expression'. It is clear they've picked a side and are committed to defending it.

Cherelle drives me home after the Pride march. Everyone in the car is a Pacific person. There is silence in the car for a moment. We are digesting the anger and the frustration. The religious people protesting at the march were Pacific people. The hardest part of standing up to them is standing up to my own people. All of this is so terribly hard. It is heart-breaking. No one teaches you how to undo generational curses. While I am struggling to navigate the racist queer community, I am burdened with the task of undoing anti-queerness in the Pacific community. The Pacific is free from the British but enslaved by Christianity.

Whether the church accepts it or not, queer Pacific people have always been here. Mahu. Vakasalewalewa. Palopa. Fa'afafine. Akava'ine. Fakaleiti. Fakafifine. Takatāpui. We are a gift from our ancestors. We don't want to be remembered as people riddled with trauma and tragedy. Anti-queer Pacific people are carrying on the work of the coloniser. I cannot imagine the amount of brainwashing it has taken for these Polynesians to come out to a Pride event and yell at queer people. I know in that moment that decolonisation ain't for the weak. My own people hate me for it.

Pride 2021 has become a dark time for the queer community. There is a spike in anti-queer violence.

Two nonbinary people are beaten in daylight for holding hands in New Plymouth. They are called homophobic slurs by a group of four. Ray Gardiner is left with a broken nose, concussion and bruising after a homophobic attack on him and his partner in Auckland. He woke up lying in a pool of his own blood. After horrific queerphobic attacks on the queer community, a group of religious bigots came to our Pride march to tell us that God hates sin. Then a Pride sign is vandalised with a 'God resists the proud' statement. On International Women's Day, a group of people gather outside the Ministry for Women to protest against trans people's right to self-identify their gender.

The queer community is under attack from the outside world when queer nightclub GAY is accused of being an unsafe space for trans people and people of colour. There have been tensions between GAY's owners, who also own neighbouring Family Bar, and staff. The tension comes to a head when Aaron Gordon is demoted from his management position for serious misconduct. Aaron says that since the new management took over, queer folk have been making complaints of being groped and of anti-social behaviour from non-queer people in the bar, and trans bar staff are being misgendered and deadnamed.

Queer people of colour stage a protest at midnight on 1 May against the owners of GAY. I am asked to speak at the event. On my way to the protest with Priyana, a Fijian trans activist messages me that Polikalepo Kefu, a Tonga *leiti*, has been murdered. Poli's battered body was found in the early hours lying at the shore. Poli was the president of the local LGBTQI+ rights group in Tonga. The Pacific queer community is shaken to the core.

Priyana and I arrive at St Kevins Arcade on Karangahape Road. The place is filling up quickly. Before we march down Karangahape Road to GAY, I take the mic and lead a chant: 'White gays wake up!' I am in a state of shock at the loss of another queer Pacific life. I am angry about the racism and transphobia in the New Zealand queer community. Filled with rage, I protest:

> We would all rather not be here, but here we are in the
> middle of the fucking night protesting just so we can
> be safe. It is 2021. I cannot believe that we are having
> to protest this shit. Trans people of colour have been
> fighting for too long to be kicked to the side when we
> are no longer needed for the liberation of white gay men.
>
> There are many white gays out tonight, but instead of
> standing here in solidarity with us, they are shaking their
> asses in one of those clubs. Trans people of colour have

been at the frontlines fighting for the rights of queer
people, but trans people are still waiting for their rights.

White gays wake up!

At the Stonewall riots, the first room to be set on fire was
the coat room. That night they burnt the closet down so
we would never have to hide again. And so, we are never
going to hide again. The world has tried to erase us, but
I am queer, and I am indigenous. My power is ancestral.
You cannot break me. Let tonight be the last night they
underestimate the power of our people.

Trans people of colour are the future. We have been
generations ahead of yesterday. Stale white males are
yesterday. We are the future. There would be no LGB
without the T, so pay some respect!

There is an uproar of 'yass' as a packed crowd clicks their fingers
and claps.

24

'Rainbow Youth Board member lashes out at "White Gays"'

This year 2021 marks 35 years since the decriminalisation of homosexuality in New Zealand. The Greens are hosting a panel called Celebrating and Reflecting: 35 Years since Homosexual Law Reform. Aaron is reinstated as manager of GAY and apologises to the club owner for the protest. A day before the panel, I receive an email inviting me to be a panellist. A speaker has pulled out, so they need a replacement. I say yes. I am speaking alongside Green MP Jan Logie, former Chief Executive Officer of Body Positive Bruce Kilmister, and CTAG member Max. Chlöe Swarbrick, Auckland Central's first openly queer MP, is facilitating our panel at Monster Valley.

One Of Them

The conversation about the criminalisation of homosexuality is difficult for me. I went into conversion therapy when I was very young, and I didn't fully realise that I was born in Fiji during a time when it was a crime to be gay. As I am preparing for the panel, I have a new realisation, and it changes how I feel about those who tried to convert me in my village. Colonisation resulted in the criminalisation of queer Pacific people, and with that came the conditioning of indigenous Pacific people, which in turn led to the conversion therapy visited on me and others.

The elders in my village knew that it was a crime to be queer when I was growing up. I have the tiniest amount of hope that maybe they were not converting me because they hated queerness — maybe they were trying to protect me from criminalisation, and they just didn't know how to protect. In the process of trying to protect me, they harmed me, but they never intended to. That does not justify their actions, but I am holding on to the hope that they didn't hate me. Indigenous Pacific peoples were conditioned with homophobia and transphobia, and they have never got a fair chance to unlearn that.

My understanding of my conversion therapy is nuanced. But I really hate this interpretation. There is no one I can blame for my suffering. The people who did this to me were functioning under a colonial mindset that they had little control over. I know it is morally wrong to punish indigenous people for acting in ways the coloniser taught them. But I really need someone to be angry at. I want to retaliate against someone.

It makes me angry and sad and frustrated, but mostly angry. Why did I deserve what they did to me? There is no one to give me an answer. I cry because I do not know what to do with these big emotions. Maturing emotionally so early — it is violent. Sometimes I want to do things that are illogical and unfair on people because they just make me feel better. Doing the right thing, trying to undo generational curses, hurts. A lot.

People see me and they hold me to the standard of a 30-year-old. They hold me to an unreasonable standard of professionalism, when all I feel like doing is lashing out. I want to be a savage. I have so much anger buried in me, burning me inside. But if I show the smallest sign of unpleasant behaviour, the entirety of the internet will be on my case. There is a bandwagon for people like me. I just want people to let me be young for once, to feel my pain and process it.

What do I do with all this anger? Where do I take it? I cannot express the pain because people will say I am weak. I cannot express anger because it makes me look hostile. Just when I think I have started healing, all that pain jumps to the surface, and it makes me so miserable.

But enough crying, it is time to suck it up and be the strong activist everyone knows me to be. I arrive at the Greens' panel.

I am the only person on the panel who's brown, trans or indigenous to the Pacific. I have to talk about the Pacific because if I don't, who else will? I know it gets annoying for some people to hear me go on and on about queer Pacific people, but hey, I am sure New Zealand queers would rather be annoyed than criminalised.

The room is packed. People are standing hard up against the wall. Chlöe introduces all the panellists. When introducing me, Chlöe reads my tweets from the morning. She reads, 'I cannot celebrate 35 years of the Homosexual Law Reform in New Zealand while so many of my people throughout the Moana are still criminals for being queer. Tonga, Samoa, Cook Islands and others continue to criminalise homosexuality. New Zealand colonised two of those islands and remains responsible for the criminalisation of queer people in those islands,' and hands the mic over to me. I am glad Chlöe referred to that tweet. It opens the conversation wide for me. I add:

> What we see is that our government has been very willing to colonise and criminalise and take advantage of indigenous peoples in the Pacific and then turn around and say, "Well, it's your fault." A lot of times, white queers make me feel I am betraying the queer community because I'm not mad at the Pacific members of Parliament who voted against gay rights. I am not mad at them. I am mad at colonisation. Sixteen-year-old me would be profusely angry at Aupito William Sio for voting against same-sex marriage but now I understand I belong to colonised peoples. White queers want to shame and dishonour the Pacific Islands and Pacific peoples for not accepting queer people, but let me remind you that it was your colonising ancestors who brought those laws onto our lands. Indigenous queerness is older than the settler state. Indigenous queerness is not a colonial consequence. You better learn that history.

On my way home from the panel, my mind is ticking. There is more I can do to create conversation about the criminalisation of queer people in the Pacific. I pick up my phone and begin to write passionately to Facebook.

> Today marks 35 years since Parliament passed a law decriminalising homosexuality but I cannot be free until all my people are free. The Homosexual Law Reform did not free me as a queer person because it did not free all queer Pacific people.

I cannot celebrate 35 years of the Homosexual Law Reform in New Zealand while so many of my people throughout the Moana are still criminals for being queer. White queers have been given a 35-year head start in equality. While the gays enjoy the freedoms of the Homosexual Law Reform in New Zealand, Queer Pacific people are still fighting for it.

Many of these white queer people are not fighting to achieve freedom for indigenous queer Pacific people. Many white queers are fighting to liberate themselves from anti-queerness so they can exercise the fullness of their white privilege. White people have been promised the world, but white queer people's queerness limits their access to their full white privilege.

White queer people have nowhere to take their anger, their frustration, their pain, and their agony in the white world. White queer people sit at the bottom of the white social hierarchy. They sit on the top of the queer social hierarchy. The only place white queer people can exercise the fullness of their white privilege is in the queer community. The day queerness ceases to be an issue for the white world, white queer people will be no different from white non-queer people.

We have waited for years for white queer people to show us solidarity and they've failed us. We cannot wait for them to save us. We have to save ourselves. We have to free ourselves.

My post sets fires through white queers' Facebook. The backlash is rife. The white queers cannot stand my audacity.

Theresa Pearson writes, 'I think this discussion should be back in the Islands from what I gather as it sounds like the problem is there.'

'Let's not get things twisted, New Zealand is a Pacific Island. And as an indigenous person, I'm more than happy to accommodate conversations for my Pacific cousins, especially if the same conversations in the other islands could get them arrested or worse,' my friend Hariata Wirihana responds.

Stephen Berry, an eight-time failed political candidate, comments, 'You're a miserable, whiney, pathetic, ungrateful racist. Those "white men" that you spit venom at fought arrest and jail so you can live the way you do now. Show some gratitude or spend a few months in Uganda — BIPOCs there will murder you in no time.'

Uganda? White people never pack their bags and leave New Zealand when they are upset at the use of te reo Māori. They complain, as Stephen is known to do, constantly.

Niccole Duval, in a long rant, left the comment, 'I suggest you learn to be a Kiwi because you're certainly not one yet.'

The Homosexual Law Reform Act did not free queer people in the Pacific Islands — that is a fact. All these white queers are angry because they know that is the truth. Maybe no one has stood up to them in the past, but I am not scared of them. I can run circles around this one-foot-in-the-grave group of dinosaurs. New Zealand wouldn't have needed a homosexual law reform Act if the British colonisers had not brought their anti-queer laws with them. So no, I refuse to accept that I am indebted to white queers. The white queers who fought to decriminalise homosexuality alongside queer and trans people of colour were fighting to undo their ancestors' wickedness. Importantly, they were not the only people fighting discriminatory laws. Queer people of colour were at the forefront.

White queer people spend more time creating lists of Black and brown majority countries where it is a crime to be gay than acknowledging the virulent racism towards Black and brown queer people in their own countries. It is easier for them to imagine the countries in which they are oppressed instead of the countries in which they are oppressive.

The white queers do not stop at leaving comments under my Facebook post. Stephen Berry creates a petition to Rainbow Youth to expel me from the Board of Rainbow Youth. Wow. Just wow. The petition reads:

> NZ Rainbow Youth: Expel racists from your board!
>
> All Individuals Matter started this petition to Rainbow Youth (Rainbow Youth Board)
>
> The signatories of this petition request that Rainbow Youth take a stand against racism by expelling Shaneel Lal from the organisation. If they refuse, then we request that all businesses donating to Rainbow Youth take a stand against racism and refuse to fund an organisation which sanctions racism.

Rainbow Youth is a support services organisation for queer youth. The white queers despise me so much, they ask businesses to withdraw money from Rainbow Youth if I am not expelled. A significant majority of people who use Rainbow Youth's services are white. If Rainbow Youth is defunded, white users will suffer the most. They hate me so much that they are willing to let queer youth go without support if that means they can get revenge. The petition adds:

Shaneel Lal, Board Member of Rainbow Youth, is a vocal racist and BIPOC supremacist. He has proudly taken steps to alter representation on the board of Rainbow Youth so that it has positions reserved for particular racial groups and even provides some racial groups with greater influence over the organisation. Rainbow Youth exists to support young gay, lesbian, bisexual, transgender etc. individuals.

I change my email signoff from 'Shaneel, Executive Board Member' to 'Shaneel, BIPOC supremacist'.

Yes, I worked tirelessly alongside the Māori and Pacific board members to secure Māori, Pacific and Asian representation on the Rainbow Youth Board. I put forward the motion to secure two seats for Māori, one seat for a Pacific person and one seat for an Asian person. I successfully passed those motions at the AGM with the support of my friends Logan Hamley, Cinnamon Lindsay and Jessee Fia'Ali'i. I will not apologise for that. I am very proud of it.

The petition goes on to claim that 'Shaneel Lal's racist crusade is warping the organisation into a racialised, extremist hate group.'

As the petition goes live, Oliver Hall, a white gay man, editor of *Gay Express*, rushes to write an article about it. *Gay Express* is run by two white gay men, Oliver and Matt Fistonich.

Oliver messages me on Facebook: 'Hi Shaneel, Express is doing a story about your comments on the 35th Anniversary of Homosexual Law Reform and the ruckus it's caused! Would you mind answering a couple of questions for me?'

'I love a witch hunt. What questions do you have?' I sarcastically reply.

Oliver replies: 'Can you confirm that you are a current Board

Member of Rainbow Youth? Do you stand by the statement you made on Facebook on 11 July regarding the 35th Anniversary of Law Reform? There is a change.org petition asking for you to be stood down from the board. Do you have any intention of standing down? The petition labels you as "racist" — do you have any comment you would like to make about that?'

I am working a part-time hospitality job on top of everything, and I have a graveyard shift tonight. Oliver is demanding answers as I am trying to prepare for work in a few hours. The stress of it all starts to bite at me, but I tell myself I cannot crack under pressure. These white queers do not deserve to see you sweat. I only have one question — 'When are you publishing?'

Oliver replies: '6:30 p.m. But I can post it now if you would rather not comment.'

6:30 p.m. is in thirty minutes. There is nothing I can say to Oliver in this moment that will paint me in a good light. I am not standing down from Rainbow Youth's board and I am not apologising to anyone. This is an orchestrated attempt to take me down.

I have risen to the top of the queer community at the speed of light. No one saw me coming, and very few are happy about my success. Most want me gone, but I am staying put right here. Cry. Throw a tantrum. Put me in a blender and turn me to soup. Run me over with a road roller. Hit me with lightning. I am not moving.

In a few minutes, an article titled 'RAINBOW YOUTH BOARD MEMBER LASHES OUT AT "WHITE GAYS"' is live on *Gay Express* magazine's website. While this article is live, *Gay Express* writes articles celebrating a young white drag performer and a young white nonbinary model.

The article reads:

Shaneel Lal's social media post on the 35th Anniversary

217

of Homosexual Law Reform has led some community members to call for their removal from the RY board.

Rainbow Youth board member Shaneel Lal took to Facebook on the 35th Anniversary of Homosexual Law Reform in New Zealand to detail why they 'cannot celebrate' the milestone, 'because it did not free all queer Pacific people.'

Comparing the law passed in New Zealand with the ongoing battle for decriminalisation of homosexuality in the Pacific, Lal claims, 'The homosexual law reform did not free me as a queer person because it did not free all queer Pacific people. I cannot celebrate 35 years of the Homosexual Law Reform in New Zealand while so many of my people throughout the Moana are still criminals for being queer.'

Lal then launched into a rant on 'white gays' . . .

Rant? Right. I am being painted as an irrational, angry, entitled, ungrateful bitchy young person. Why am I 'ranting' and not raising valid concerns about racism in the queer community? This is what they do to people of colour who stand up to the status quo. They portray us as troublemakers.

The article concludes by hyperlinking the petition against me. Oliver knows that doing so will promote the petition against me for more people to sign. The article says: 'A change.org petition has also now been launched calling for Lal's removal from Rainbow Youth.

It is 11 p.m. and I am on a fifteen-minute break at my hospitality job. I open Facebook and see the article is now posted to the

Express Magazine Facebook page. I am thinking about what I should do. There is not much I can do on a fifteen-minute break.

Grant Allen comments on the article, misgendering me:

> This person Shaneel Lal has managed to insult and
> denigrate so many people in his FB stream. People who did
> the hard yards and created a situation where he has been
> enabled to have a platform to megaphone from. I'd like to
> see this racist narcissist carry on in Fiji as he has been here,
> he'd be in jail in a flash. Definitely signing the petition. He's
> toxic and should not be in any position where he is seen as
> a role model for vulnerable youth.

Karen Ritchie replies, misgendering me, 'Grant Allen agree! But that can always be a two-way street. How does he think it has affected some of my transgender friends who are in their 70s feel who he totally insulted on his public post. He needs to learn respect and if it's the hard way so be it.'

I can't believe *Gay Express* managed to find a literal Karen to comment on me. Karen adds, still misgendering me, 'He is toxic and needs to learn respect or shut his mouth.' I have to go back to work. I finish work at seven the next morning and go straight to bed when I get home.

I wake to emails from the Executive Director of Rainbow Youth and some board members. They are supportive of me, but they choose to remain silent about the article. To the public it looks like Rainbow Youth is choosing not to defend me. It is not long before the tides turn, however. The article against me is not received as *Gay Express* wished. Their article gets slammed on Facebook by over 500 people. Change.org steps in and deletes the petition against me, saying that the petition is transphobic and intentionally misgenders me.

Stephen creates a second petition and notes, 'Karen Ritchie and many other LGBT activists have asked me to start a new petition requesting Shaneel Lal step down from the board of Rainbow Youth. I'm honoured to do so.' Honoured? If I ran a petition against another person and only received 299 signatures, I would be embarrassed not honoured.

One commentator writes, 'They've done more for the community without [Mr Gay New Zealand], I think they were disappointed-but-not-surprised, then moved on to more productive uses of their time.'

Another adds, 'I don't understand why it's OK to publish this but to not publish an article that investigates inequities within our community prior to this. Would have been great to see our community media facilitating this a bit more rather than reactionary reporting like this. Shaneel is right. Also, NOT moderating comments which misgender Shaneel is disgusting.'

Auckland Pride Festival, Wellington Pride Festival, Qtopia and other queer organisations start releasing statements of support for me. My friend and fellow board member Cinnamon Lindsay sees that all queer organisations except Rainbow Youth are making public statements to support me and condemn *Gay Express*. Cinnamon writes to the board:

> I think RY should make a public statement, whether we like it or not this is in the public sphere, and we should tautoko Shaneel in a way that is tangible. Auckland Pride Festival has released a statement and I think we need to show the same manaaki for one of our beautiful, powerful, outspoken members. We have the facts, we can back everything up and if they are receiving death threats and fake messages (someone made a fake email for Logan and emailed

Shaneel that they were let go from the board) then we need to make it known that this is not okay.

I don't think our silence honours what Shaneel has said and what we stand for.

Rainbow Youth come together in an instant after Cinnamon's email and release a public statement in which they write:

Shaneel Lal has been pivotal to our growth as an organisation. Over the last two board terms, they have been invaluable in building connections that help us better serve communities we were unable to connect with in the past and guiding us closer to our aspiration of supporting all rainbow young people. We have been fortunate to have people like Shaneel provide their insight, passion and commitment to RainbowYOUTH.

After this statement, while the old white queers are still begging people to withdraw money from Rainbow Youth, we start receiving donations in my name. We receive over $2000.

I am deeply grateful for Cinnamon's friendship and advocacy for me. I have felt so alone in the queer community for so long. And it sucked. I need this. I know I am strong, but I have always presented myself as tougher than I wanted to be or felt inside. I am only 21, and I am being constantly attacked. The brighter I shine, the faster people want me to burn, but stars do not burn out fast.

I was praying for a soft chapter in life, and things only got harder. I do not want people to think that I am going to accept bullying. I put on a strong face and fire back. *Gay Express* is drowning in comments of support and condemnation for me on Facebook and

Instagram.

Gay Express quietly deletes their article. Neither Oliver Hall nor Matt Fistonich apologise to me. I write a petition asking *Gay Express* to issue a public apology. When I get 1,000 signatures, I write to Oliver, 'The petition you shared in your article was held to be transphobic by change.org. You wrote about a petition that received 40 signatures in days. I have received more than 1,000 signatures in less than 5 hours. Surely this is of enough public interest to get an article of its own.'

The petition quickly garners 2,700 signatures. Oliver opens my message but does not respond. Facebook does, though, and says, 'You can't message Oliver. You can't message or call in this chat, and you won't receive their messages or calls.' Oliver has blocked me. Coward! I refuse to be bullied by white gay men. My life has become about standing up. I stood up to Jack, I stood up to the church leader who tried to convert me at Middlemore Hospital. I stood up to the church members who came to protest at Pride. I am standing up to the state to ban conversion therapy. Oliver is nothing.

My second term on the Rainbow Youth Board is coming to an end. I am elected to serve another two years as board member. A few weeks later I am elected to the board of Auckland Pride Festival and appointed a trustee of Adhikaar Aotearoa, a charity that provides education, support and advocacy for queer South Asians. Not a word from *Gay Express*. I get the last laugh.

25
Burning out

We are nearing the middle of 2021. The Labour party will introduce the bill to ban conversion therapy anytime now. I am set to speak at the Festival for the Future in Wellington on 1 August on the importance of banning conversion therapy, and I am leaving for Wellington on 28 July. The Labour party is not telling me when they will make their proposed bill public. I have not been consulted by the Ministry of Justice, so I do not know what the Minister will put forward.

On the night of 27 July, a Labour staffer leaks the Minister of Justice's press release on the Conversion Practices Prohibition Legislation Bill to me. The cheek, the nerve, the gall, the audacity and the gumption of the Minister to put forward this bill. I am appalled at its quality. I try not to be angry. When I am angry, I get so worked up that I cannot focus on doing anything. I must stay calm and put my strategic mind at play. How do I make this leak work in my favour?

I have so many questions. Why did the Labour party keep all this information from me until this point? I am not an outsider to them. I started my journey to ban conversion therapy as a Labour party youth MP. I spoke to almost everyone on the Labour backbench regularly. All of them adore me (or at least I think they do) and treat me like a friend. I met with the Deputy Chair of the Justice Select Committee, Vanushi Walters, to discuss how I could support the

Labour party during the select committee process. I met with Kris to advise him on the direction of the Bill despite being kept out of the Ministry of Justice's consultation. I was like a part of their party.

Everything the Labour party tries to keep from me gets sent to me before they can release the information to the public. They underestimate the friendship between young people in politics. It is the young Labour staffers who leak this information to me. We didn't enter politics for the theatrics and fame. We entered the political arena because we wanted to create change. They inform me that the Minister of Justice is introducing the Bill to Parliament and doing a press conference on 30 July at the New Zealand AIDS Foundation Headquarters in St Marys Bay, Auckland.

I immediately contact Labour MP Shanan Halbert and ask him if the Labour party is introducing the Bill on 30 July. I don't tell him I have seen the press release and the bill. He does not deny it. My phone rings, and it is Shanan calling. He invites me to the press conference at the New Zealand AIDS Foundation.

I am leaving for Wellington in the morning for the next five days. I change my flights to leave in the evening on 30 July after the Labour party's press conference. I am irritated at this constant last-minute run-around. The Labour party does something, I find out, I investigate and then they invite me to be a part of it. By then it is impossible to be involved. Working with them is like herding cats. If the Labour party wanted me to be at the conference, they would have told me ahead of time so that I could be there. They did not. They were not expecting me to find out this information before their press conference. If the information was not leaked to me, I would be oblivious to their release and on my flight to Wellington.

I cannot let the Labour party keep treating me like this. I draft a post about their proposed bill. I write comprehensive criticism of it before they can release it. I know the exact time the Labour party is going live with their press release and the Bill on 30 July. Since I am no longer flying out to Wellington on the 28th, I go to university in the morning. I am sitting in my public law class waiting for the Bill to be announced, restless and impatient. I refresh the Minister of Justice's website every few seconds. The student sitting behind me is probably wondering why I have been refreshing the same website for an hour.

As soon as my class finishes, I rush to my usual study room in the psychology department. I am not heading to the psychology building to study. Every time I go to type something, I press the wrong buttons. I am having an out of body experience from the sudden spike of adrenaline in my body. My mouth is producing unreasonable amounts of saliva. I need to calm myself down before the announcement goes live.

I know exactly what is coming, but I am still nervous. One more refresh button and there is a new announcement on the top. It gives my restless heart and mind another boost of adrenaline. My mind is out of control. At the same time the Labour party goes live with their press release on the New Zealand Government's website, I post my drafted post to Instagram. My post about the Bill is the first on social media. I steal Labour's thunder and take control of the narrative. It's what they deserve.

The Labour party is parading their bill as the best in the world. That is simply not the case. My Instagram post and tweets gain traction, and my phone begins to ring. I know I have to tell the media everything that needs to be changed about this bill. Jenna Lynch from *Newshub* calls me, and I tell her that it will remain legal to practise conversion therapy on an eighteen-year-old as long as you do not cause them serious harm. That is the reality. The Labour party is proposing to make conversion therapy a criminal offence to perform on a person under the age of eighteen. But if the victim is eighteen years old or older, conversion therapy is only a crime if the victim suffers 'serious' harm. This means that people can practise conversion therapy on an eighteen-year-old and cause them harm and that will remain legal. Why is the Labour party doing this? Why are they leaving eighteen-year-olds without protection?

I am most concerned about section 12 of the Bill. Section 12 says there will be no prosecutions without the Attorney General's consent. The Attorney General is a member of the government of the day. This bill gives the Attorney General the absolute power to determine whether a case will be prosecuted or not; in other words, the ban on conversion practices is at the mercy of the attorney general of the day. If a government that does not support this ban comes into power, the ban on conversion practices ceases. The National party has been clear that it will not criminalise parents for stopping trans children from being trans. A queerphobic attorney general or an attorney general of a government that does not support a ban can simply refuse to prosecute all cases under this ban and immediately render it useless.

1 News asks to interview me and the Minister of Justice. The Minister is interviewed first and says that the intent of the Bill is not to criminalise people. It is to prevent harm. I point out that the Labour party is not offering any financial support for victims and survivors of conversion therapy to seek mental health support. I ask the Minister to cover mental harm suffered as a result of conversion therapy in ACC. He declines my request through a media interview. The Minister and I are having a conversation through media interviews. It is comical. I have to see him in less than an hour for the press conference.

The Labour party is confused about how I developed comprehensive criticisms of their bill within minutes of their announcement. They do not know that I had seen their bill a few days earlier. They aren't ready to respond to the concerns I raise to the media. Suddenly everything makes sense. The Labour party is putting forward a toothless bill. It makes sense now why they didn't want me to know ahead of time. The Ministry of Justice kept me out of their consultations so they could plausibly say they were unaware of my concerns when I criticised their bill. I wouldn't have been able to articulate my concerns clearly and confidently if today had been the first time I'd seen the bill.

After doing my media interviews, I arrive at the New Zealand AIDS Foundation building. The room is full of Labour MPs and New Zealand AIDS Foundation and OutLine Aotearoa staff. Shanan hugs me and takes me into the crowd. I have spent all morning ripping their bill to shreds in the media, and yet I walk in like we have all been holding hands and singing 'Kumbaya' leading up to this moment. To my surprise, there is no awkwardness. I think the very strange cornerstone of politics is that you can adore the people while feeling deeply frustrated by the policies they're championing. I struggle with it. I have not figured out how to balance my disdain for the Labour party's bill to ban conversion therapy with my love for many of the Labour MPs. Marja, Terisa Ngobi and Angela Roberts are present too. They are some of kindest Labour MPs I know. I feel more at ease knowing they are here.

The Labour party ask me to sit with them in their press conference. I giggle. The journalists who have interviewed me a few minutes ago are present at the press conference. They know that I am not happy with the Bill. I agree to join them. Minister Faafoi and Shanan sit in the front row. I sit in the second row with Marja, Terisa and Angela. I am in clear view of the camera as my head bops between Minister Faafoi and Shanan. Minister Faafoi gives the details of the Bill to the media. After the press conference, I rush back home to South Auckland, pack my bags and head to the airport. I am going to Wellington to speak at the Festival of the Future.

I feel like I have forgotten something, but I can't tell what. I get to the airport, and I realise I forgot my facewash at home. There is no way I am leaving Auckland without my skincare. I have planned to see Neihana tonight, who is now working in Wellington after graduating. I call Neihana and as soon as he picks up, I yell, 'Hey, can you go and buy me a Neutrogena Pink Grapefruit Oil-Free Acne Wash before the supermarkets close? I forgot my facewash at home, and I need it tonight.' Neihana agrees immediately. I am surprised he does not ask any questions or make any excuses.

Neihana buys the facewash. He sends me a picture and now I can get on the plane in peace. I meet Neihana at Ivy Bar. I have not seen him since the Labour party won the election. Now the Labour party has introduced their bill to ban conversion therapy. We have come a long way.

I run at Neihana when I see him and jump in for a hug. It is time to dance like we did at GAY.

I return to my hotel room late and I am shattered from attending university, speaking to media, meeting politicians, flying to Wellington and shaking my ass with Neihana at Ivy. I have to speak at the Festival for the Future in less than two days, and I have not perfected my speech yet. My eyes are fighting to shut, but I start practising my speech for the festival. I am determined to make the most of every minute. I am knocked out the moment my head hits the bed.

The next morning, I cannot stop laughing.

I wake up and find the live stream of the press conference from yesterday. My friend has sent me screenshots of the video, and I look mortified in them. It looks like I don't want to be there.

I was upset with the Labour party's bill but nothing so serious had happened that required me to make faces like I was on an episode of *Real Housewives*. I can see the exact moment I begin to dissociate from the physical realm and enter an alternative universe. I roll in bed laughing. I can control my mouth, but my face? I take no responsibility. My face has a mind of its own.

I arrive at the TSB Arena at the Wellington waterfront in a brown turtleneck and baby blue suit. For once, I am not nervous. I feel comfortable. I've done these enough times. I feel great right after my talk at the Festival for the Future. I think I impressed the crowd. When I get off the stage with the other speakers, there is a line of people waiting for me. Uh oh. I do not think I have the energy to talk to so many people about the same thing. Some people ask for photos. This is a new experience for me. I am in a politician's utopia. But I am not a politician. It is the first time I grasp the kind of influence I have.

My energy dwindles after each encounter. It is so repetitive; it becomes a chore. My arms swing by my side and then they stop swinging altogether. My eyelids feel heavier, and my feet slap the ground harder as I walk. My shoulders sink deeper into my chest. I am giving everyone a cross-eyed stare. As I walk out of the auditorium towards the food stalls, groups of people approach me to talk to me about my speech. I have to make a five-minute stop every two steps.

It takes me forever to get out of the auditorium and to the food stalls. I pick up some bread, and head to the table where Brianna is sitting. As I turn around, people surround me and start talking to me about politics. I will drop dead any moment now. I feel like I am stuck in Auckland traffic at 5 p.m. I hyperfocus on the people in front of me, and everything else is a blur. Normally, talking to a crowd is my thing, but today, I want to run away and hide from people. I cannot understand this need to avoid people.

I don't think I am being antisocial. I like people, but I feel so fatigued, I struggle to smile at them. Nothing is helping me. I try to nap, eat, and get fresh air and I still feel the same. I tell Brianna that the next time someone tries to talk to me and it goes on for too long, to come and say we are running late for the next event. More people come, and Brianna employs our strategy. I run outside with Brianna and sit on the wooden railing looking out to the waterfront. The water is a jewel-blue paradise. It quivers and sparkles in the bright sun. I look up to see fluffy white lines in the sky like a plane just flew by. Squawking gulls squabble in the distance. I am relieved they are not nearby to harass me. The waves are rippling gently against the railings under my feet. I stare at it with numbness. The briny air is fighting to open my droopy eyes.

I am the ocean's child. I grew up by the water. The ocean puts my heart at ease. I want it to recharge me, but I feel like a drained battery that can no longer hold its charge. The things that always made me happy no longer have any effect on me. It seeps into my mind, but there is nothing to welcome it. My indifference to the pulsing heart of the water frightens me. I am burning out.

26
Burnt out

I feel like a dry teapot over a high flame. There are good things happening in my life, but nothing makes me feel happy. I am empty inside. It is like trying to fill a strainer. I feel numb to everything that is happening around me. I have drained myself trying to lead this movement. I am past the burning out phase; I am habitually burnt out. I am in a vibrant relationship with anxiety and depression.

I wake up and promise myself that today will be different. I will do work today. All I have to do is follow a routine and I will be able to complete my work. I wake up early, sit on my bed, place my laptop on a chair and turn it on. The phrase 'I will get work done today' replays in my head. My laptop turns on, and I pout as my eyes well up. All the blood flowing in my face makes me red, puffy and strained. I feel no motivation to watch my lectures, write my assignments or reply to my emails.

I reach for my phone to call Frederic only to remember I can't. How did I forget he isn't around anymore? I feel so alone. I do not like whatever I am experiencing. I feel like someone has punched me in the gut wearing steel gloves. It feels like losing him all over again, like I have just read his sister's post on his Facebook. I curl up in bed with my pillow. I want to stay like this forever. Everything feels out of my control.

No one told me that trying to lead a political movement would be this exhausting and working with politicians this frustrating. I have university to attend, my hospitality job to work, relationships to maintain and this movement to run. My grades are suffering. I can't seem to get interested in university. My friendships are breaking down. I fear opening messages. I do not have the energy to commit to a catch-up, so I do not open the messages, only to reply a week later saying I am so sorry for replying so late. I make every excuse to avoid seeing people. I have to work because I have bills to pay.

In true New Zealand politics fashion, on 4 August a Labour staffer messages me: 'The conversion therapy bill will have its first reading tomorrow.'

What? I cannot believe it. The Labour party has the first reading of the Conversion Practices Prohibition Legislation Bill without any communication with grassroots activists or survivors of conversion therapy. It is common to let the public know ahead of time. The Parliament gallery overflowed with supporters for the third reading of the bill to allow same-sex marriage. Politicians want supporters of their bill to flood Parliament. It feels unreal that there is no desire to have us in the gallery.

I am in Auckland, and the first reading of the Bill is happening tomorrow in Wellington. I cannot drop everything and leave for Wellington hours before the first reading. I don't have an abundance of money sitting around to book an expensive last-minute flight and hotel in Wellington. I cannot go. I cannot be there for the first reading of the bill I worked so hard to get into the House because the Labour party did not give me a heads-up. I am not welcome. I have found out through yet another leak.

I want to return to bed. The dreadful feeling is still residing in me. But I have to do something with this information. I sluggishly pick up my phone to share the information with everyone. I tweet: 'Tomorrow, 5 August after 3 p.m. New Zealand Parliament will vote on the Conversion Practices Prohibition Legislation Bill for the first time. If you can make it to Parliament, please do! This is a monumental day in the movement to end conversion therapy.'

On first reading day, things hit rock-bottom. The Young Nats share that the National party is voting against banning conversion therapy. This is a complete surprise. I was under the impression that the National party would vote in favour of the Bill as Judith Collins promised. But on the day of the first reading, she announces that she and the National party are against the ban. Judith tweets, 'National is very clear that we must not criminalise parents for offering advice to their children, nor objecting to puberty blockers being given to their children. Labour needs to amend its legislation before we will support it.'

Judith is more volatile as the leader of the National party than is the economy during a global pandemic. No one knows what to expect from her.

There are seven steps to a bill becoming a law. It is introduced into Parliament at first reading. If the bill passes, it goes to a select committee. MPs come together at the select committee to amend the bill and to address any concerns they have about it. It then goes to second reading for a second round of voting. MPs who vote in favour of the bill at the first reading can, and do, vote against the bill at the second reading if they are unsatisfied with it after the select committee process. After the second reading there is the Committee of the Whole House, where MPs can amend the bill through Supplementary Order Papers. The bill then goes to the third and final reading. It becomes law when it passes third reading and receives royal assent from the Governor General. The bill to ban conversion therapy is just at first reading and it is already facing obstacles.

I message Chris Bishop. Chris met me in February and told me that I could trust him to have my back. Surely, he will not be voting against the ban on conversion therapy. Chris does not reply. He normally tweets an annoying amount. He has not tweeted anything since Judith has announced that the National party will vote against banning conversion therapy. My suspicions feel right. Chris, too, is voting against the ban despite telling me he is an ally to queer people.

I sit in my room with my laptop to watch the speeches. I am alone. CTAG did not get an opportunity to plan a get-together. My heart is beating like a drum in my chest in anticipation of the speeches. It only gets faster as the time gets closer. I am sweating. I feel like I am on fire, the flames starting deep in the pit of my stomach. I clench my jaw, wring my hands and tap my feet incessantly. But the minute that Minister Faafoi gets up to officially introduce the Bill to the house, I take control of my breathing. I am not happy with the Labour party's bill, but after the crazy day I've had, I feel comforted that the Labour party has a majority in Parliament and there is nothing the National party can do to stop this ban. The only thing that National MPs are about to do is make fools of themselves.

The National MPs give their speeches. They insist they want to see conversion therapy banned and they want to work with the Government to amend the Bill. However, they vote against the Government's bill at the first reading. MPs only vote against bills at the first reading to prevent it from going to the select committee. If the National party wants to work with the Government to amend the Bill, then why aren't they voting in favour of it at first reading to send it to select committee where they can amend it?

The National party either thinks that New Zealanders are unaware of parliamentary processes, or they don't know the parliamentary processes themselves. They are attempting to fool New Zealanders, but it is blatantly clear to everyone that the National party is playing political football with queer lives. National MPs saying 'We absolutely condemn conversion therapy' and 'There's no place for conversion therapy in New Zealand' but then voting against banning conversion therapy is the most performative and manipulative politicking I've seen.

Even the Young Nats understand the parliamentary processes. They tweet that they believe the National caucus 'should commit to supporting it through the first reading and follow through by proposing workable amendments to the concerns raised.'

The night progresses with robust debate. Every time a National MP gets up to explain why they are voting against the ban, anger floods my veins. My knuckles whiten and I gently punch the chair my laptop is sitting on. I feel irritated just looking at the smug faces of these National MPs. They have no idea what conversion therapy does to people. I cannot listen to this filth anymore. I mute my laptop. I suffered for years in conversion therapy. I tried to kill myself because of it. But this fury is pointless. The National party cannot stop the ban.

At the end of the speeches, Deputy Speaker of the House Adrian Rurawhe puts the Bill for the House to vote. He says, 'Those of that opinion will say "Aye".'

The Labour, Green, Māori party and ACT MPs say 'Aye'.

Adrian continues: 'To the contrary, "No".'

A quiet voice from the National party says 'No.'

Adrian declares that 'The ayes have it.'

The National party calls for a party vote.

Kieran McAnulty on behalf of the Labour party gives '65 votes in favour.'

Joseph Mooney jumps out of his seat on behalf of the National party to record their '33 votes opposed.'

Greens, Te Pāti Māori and ACT vote in favour.

Adrian reads, 'Members, the ayes are 87, the noes are 33.'

The Bill passes first reading. There is applause in the House. I close my laptop and fall back on my bed. I feel a childlike vulnerability in this moment, like I am lost in a supermarket aisle and I cannot find my parents. I am transported back to the temples in Fiji. I sit back up on my bed, hugging my knees. A gut-wrenching sob tears through my chest. I chew on my bottom lip to make myself stop but once the first tear leaves my eyes, it is impossible for me to stop. It is beyond my control now.

I try to breathe normally but someone is clutching me, stopping me from taking full breaths. My heart is about to break my ribcage and burst out at any moment. Trembling, I rest the side of my forehead on my knees. My forearms keep slipping down my knees. I feel the sinister presence of the elders and my teachers around me. The monumental moment for the movement does not bring me joy. It suffocates me and puts me back in the memories I have been trying to escape. I keep running away from the things that happened to me, but they always catch up. These wracking memories were never processed and filed away. They are lying around loose in my mind. It is why I keep moving. I never stop to rest.

I am no longer in the temple in my village; I am not in the chapel of my school. I am safe, but my mind won't believe it. My mind thinks there is danger lurking around somewhere about to get me. My mind gets the ball rolling. 'I am not safe, I am not safe, I am not safe,' it chants.

My phone is exploding with buzzes. The screen lights up with messages of congratulations. I am getting many phone calls, but I do not answer them. I have to do one thing. I need to post my drafted post about the passing of the Bill. I open Instagram, post my draft and close the app. My followers are filling the comment section. I don't know when I fall asleep.

The sun is beaming through my curtain. I groan and turn my

face to the other side. My phone rings. It triggers a throbbing headache. I place one hand on my head and pick the phone up. It is a journalist. My voice is still deep from the drowsiness. My body feels heavy and my muscles paralysed. I imagine this is how one's body feels after a very long night at the gym.

I am in the present, though.

Despite National's last-minute attempt to stifle the queer community last night, the Conversion Practices Prohibition Legislation Bill passed its first reading with 87 votes in favour. The words '33 votes opposed' are etched in my mind. I cannot explain why those words have stayed with me, but they have. Maybe it is the utter shock that there are 33 members of Parliament in 2021 publicly voting against the humanity of queer people.

Maintaining their strong record of voting against queer rights, the entire National party voted against banning conversion therapy. Yes, even the supposed socially progressive National MPs like Erica Stanford, Chris Bishop and Nicola Willis voted to keep conversion therapy legal in New Zealand. There are no real allies in the National party. They say they have your back, but when the time comes to act on their allyship, time and time again they show us their true colours. National MPs acquiesced to Judith to protect their place in their party. They are not allies. They are photo-op-seeking politicians.

Chris's vote maddens me the most. After voting against banning conversion therapy he tweets, 'I strongly support banning conversion therapy. That is National's position too. Our caucus has determined we can't support this bill in its current form. I am confident parliament can improve the law so we can support the bill into law.'

I have had enough of Chris trying to claim he is an ally while voting against a law that will protect us from practices that seek to erase us. I tweet back: 'You are an awful person. You looked at me and said I could trust you and you assured me you were an ally. You lied to me. I was a fool for trusting a National MP. You are not an ally. I stop you from calling yourself an ally. You have no right to call yourself an ally.'

Later that day Chris sent a Twitter-user a message and it did not go as planned.

> Chris: 'Enjoyed your piece in the law talk.'
> Twitter user: 'Thanks, Chris. Hated your vote on conversion therapy.'
> Chris: 'Yeah. Me too.'
> Twitter user: 'Clearly not enough to cross the floor, eh.'

Five days later Judith declares the Conversion Practices Prohibition Legislation Bill anti-parents and Simon Bridges adds that this bill is stopping parents from being parents. Judith says that she will not support a bill that will criminalise parents for being parents. They are both immensely supportive of parents who object to puberty blockers and stop trans children from being trans. Judith and Simon just do not get it. Conversion therapy is not good parenting. If your hate for queer people erodes your love for your children, you are not a good parent. Is it anti-parents to not allow parents to push their children to the point that they want to kill themselves?

Little does Judith know that the government already tells parents how to parent their children. The anti-smacking laws were introduced in New Zealand to stop parents from beating their children. The anti-conversion practices law extends those protections to prevent psychological harm. There is so much information about the harm done by conversion therapy at this point. There are stories of victims and survivors whose lives were destroyed by conversion therapy. Judith chooses to ignore all of it.

The national debate is taking an anti-trans turn as Judith and Simon come in defence of parents who want to stop their trans children from being trans. I try to combat their misinformation by putting out as much educational material as I can on Instagram, Facebook and Twitter. The debate is heated, and I am determined to win this one.

The Justice Select Committee opens for submissions on the Conversion Practices Prohibition Legislation Bill seven days after it passes the first reading. Between the passing of the Bill and the select committee, I've had no time to prepare. All my time has been wasted debating Chucky and her minions.

I have university and work too. I have forgotten that other commitments exist. The only thing I think about is banning conversion therapy. It's become my personality. I am too afraid of talking about anything other than politics and creating change. People might think that I am not doing all I can to get this law over the line. I cannot have people thinking that I am resting while I could be replying to questions, making social media content and writing emails to politicians. They most certainly cannot see me having fun amid this campaign. What would people think? I am dancing while conversion therapy is legal? No. I need people to think I am seriously committed to this movement. I will post about *me* after this movement is over.

Oh, God. There is just so much left to do, and I am already knackered. I do not have the time to explain to every person how select committees work. I just do not. I do not have time to teach every individual what to write in their submission, what part of the law to criticise, what to keep, what to remove.

I have not prepared any guides or templates for the queer community or allies to use for the select committee submissions.

One Of Them

The process has run me over. It is moving fast, and if I do not start running faster, I will be a victim of a dragging death. I am hardly done with the last part when the next hits me. I know it will be an onerous task to get enough submissions in favour of banning conversion therapy while combating the misinformation the right-wingers and the church will propagate.

On 17 August 2021, just when the Justice Select Committee opens for submissions on the Conversion Practices Prohibition Legislation Bill, New Zealand detects its first community case of the Delta variant of Covid-19. After 100 days of no community transmissions of Covid-19, we are hit with an Alert Level 4 lockdown. I spiral — how am I going to get enough submissions while in complete lockdown?

27
Megachurches on the attack

The end date of the select committee submissions races towards me without mercy as I stare at an empty screen. I have never made a submission to Parliament on any bill before. It is not really imposter syndrome I am feeling. I genuinely do not know how the process works. I do not know what to write in my submission. I have to learn how to do it, and after I do that, I have to teach everyone else who is waiting for direction from me. A large group of the movement's supporters are heavily reliant on me. I have to tell them exactly how to make submissions and exactly what to say. Many of these people have never made a submission before either. I understand it is difficult for them to engage with the select committee process.

Nothing comes to mind. I stare at my keyboard with an empty mind. But the longer I take, the larger advantage the churches will gain on queer people. Megachurches are prepared to campaign, and they are mobilising thousands of people to submit for an exemption to practise religious conversion therapy.

Arise Church vocally opposes passing the Conversion Practices Prohibition Legislation Bill as proposed by the Government. Paul Cameron of Arise Church leads the opposition. On 30 August, he appeals to the church's entire membership in a video, to make submissions to the Justice Select Committee and call on them to make exemptions for religious people and parents.

After sending the video, Arise Church posts an update on their website about the Bill. They write: '. . . This bill goes too far. In its effort to protect young people it has shattered the rights of parents to guide their children, counsellors and pastors to pray for young people and even for young people themselves to seek the help they want.'

I find Arise Church so dramatic for using the sentence 'shattered the rights of parents to guide their children'. Arise Church pretending that young queer children just walk into conversion therapy fully consenting and with understanding as to what it means for them is ignorant at best. No one goes into conversion therapy without coercion from church, family and society. Arise Church's post continues:

> To explain further, the bill in its current form makes it a crime — punishable by a prison sentence — to help a child dealing with sexuality or gender issues if the intention is to 'change or suppress the child's sexual orientation, gender identity, or gender expression,' even if the child or teenager gives consent! This point is worth repeating — if a teenager or child genuinely wants help to deal with issues or feelings and they want to bring about change, it will be illegal for anyone to help them achieve this goal!
> This means parents can't encourage their own children to consider all options, provide honest parental advice, or discuss past traumatic issues that may have led to confusion and questioning.

Even with well-documented evidence that conversion therapy

triples suicide rates and severe depression and no evidence that conversion therapy ever works, Arise Church's want young people to go into conversion therapy if they give 'consent'! Young queer people won't have 'issues or feelings' to 'deal with' and 'want to bring about change' if churches don't their head with the garbage idea that queerness is sinful, and that they will burn in Hell if they don't change. Young queer people do not need the church to 'help' them. They need the church to leave them alone.

When the elders first told me that I needed to change, the only thought running through my head was how I could ever survive without my family. How will I ever survive on the streets? Fear nearly consumed me. It flooded my veins. I trusted the elders like they were God. I thought they were there to protect me from the evil. In my mind, I had no real choice. I was a kid. The elders knew that I was merely a kid. I knew of nothing outside my family, village and school.

As I took the whippings on my back, all I prayed for was change. They could have beaten me to death, and I still would've prayed for change. There was no choice. There was no consent. There was only fear and deception. The elders abused my trust and their power put me through hell, the very thing they promised to protect me from. Years after escaping them, the trauma they inflicted on me follows me.

Arise Church does not have a clue what I went through.

They demand that the law is amended to add a section that reads, 'In this Act, conversion practice does not include respectful and open discussions regarding sexuality and gender, and advice, guidance, prayer, or support given to anyone by anyone else including parents, family members, friends, counsellors, religious leaders, or health professionals, when such advice or support is requested and is respectful and non-coercive.'

Arise Church's proposal will keep conversion therapy legal for parents, family members, friends, counsellors, religious leaders or health professionals if they can somehow construe children's submission to authority as consent.

I am in my room, like I have been for most of the year. I have felt every emotion known to mankind in this room, but I have mostly felt anger. I burn with outrage as I witness Arise Church's campaign to keep most forms of conversion therapy legal.

The churches have the upper hand. They have thousands of followers throughout the country, and it takes just one email to reach them all. My social media following does not amount to a quarter of the number of people in their churches. Arise Church can outweigh all the submissions I am gathering from social media with just one email. Arise Church has money. A lot of it. They can make videos, host events, run ads. I cannot do any of that. My job is cut out for me.

I have to finish my personal submission. I have to finish CTAG's submission. I have to write instructions on the submission process. I have to write templates that other people can use for their submissions. I have to convince people to make the submissions. I have to put content on social media to combat the misinformation from the churches. Bloody hell, I am damned. I ask the chair of the Justice Select Committee, Ginny Anderson, to give us more time to get our submissions in. She declines our request for an extension.

The churches ramp up their opposition. Seventeen churches sign a letter written by Tak Bhana of Church Unlimited and send it out to all their members encouraging them to make submissions to the select committee. The opposition has lifted from one church with thousands of members to seventeen churches with hundreds of thousands. The letter is signed by churches including Arise Church, Life, Curate Church, Equippers Churches and City

Impact Church. I am up against mammoths. That email argues that the Bill limits the freedoms of parents to counsel their children, the Bill is unclear about what would be legal and illegal, and the Bill limits people's freedoms to seek prayer and counselling and the churches' freedoms to provide it.

A part of the email stands out to me. It reads:

> I want to say as genuinely and lovingly as I can that questions around identity, such as sexual orientation and gender, are really sensitive and should be handled with the utmost care and compassion. Every single person experiencing questions or struggles in these areas should know they are: Deeply loved by God and fundamentally no worse or better than anyone else seeking God's mercy. Deeply loved and welcome in our church family.

It feels so familiar to how I was treated by the Hindu priests and the Christian Church growing up in Fiji. The religious leaders and priests told me they loved me. They said they were protecting me.

As a former churchgoer I am well aware of the cunning and devious ways in which the church works. I am familiar with the statements that begin with showing pretend care and love for the queer community before attacking our humanity. These statements of support are often opening statements that position religious extremists as reasonable people rather than who they really are, bigots. Religious leaders liberate themselves from their history of repeated anti-queer actions every time there is a new debate on queer rights. They get a clean slate each time even though their hands are muddied with a history of hatred against people like me.

We must look at the present actions of these churches in the context of their past actions. It is vital that people are aware that these religious leaders are not reasonable people agreeing to disagree on topics. Instead, they are a group of people with an anti-queer agenda. It illuminates something important. Christians want to have a say on everything: conversion therapy, same-sex marriage, abortion, anti-smacking laws and any other issue that affects a vulnerable group. Has anyone ever stopped to question what expertise, if any, the church has on any of these matters?

Why do we treat the voice of church leaders as though they have the same level of understanding of pseudoscientific practices as medical professionals do? While all medical bodies oppose conversion therapy, call it unethical and support banning it, the churches are being treated as though their view could somehow disprove the findings of the medical professionals.

We need to stop listening to religious extremists in conversations about human rights. Giving equal weight to misinformation and anti-queer bigotry as to the years of hard work by medical professionals is a disservice to the people who have committed themselves to providing reliable and trustworthy information.

The select committee process is wrecking my mind. I am trying to find my way through a daunting, elitist system without any guidance from anyone. I was thrown into the lion's den. Perhaps I walked right into it. It's not like I had choices. I know I had to mobilise the community to make submissions to the Justice Select Committee. I know that if I do not do it, people will tell me I failed the community. I have to do this, and I have to do most of it alone.

At about 3 a.m., a week overdue, Harry Robson, a member of CTAG, reaches out to support me. Harry is like a lifebelt. I exhale a huge pent-up breath while holding a hand over my chest and fall back on my bed. I get up and run to the kitchen to fetch a glass of water. Then I dive on my bed again. I cannot describe how much pressure it takes off me to have someone else take some of the responsibility. We Zoom each other and start working CTAG's submission. Harry takes responsibility of finishing and submitting CTAG's submission, so I can focus on getting community submissions.

I write the templates, put them on a Google Doc with instructions on how to submit, create a Linktree, post the Linktree to Instagram and go straight to bed. I don't know what kind of response I will get, but my back hurts too much from all the slouched sitting I have done in the last week to care.

My alarm terrorises me a few hours later. It's a bomb going off in my ear. Eyes still glued together, I rush to open Instagram. There are over 20,000 likes, and 4,500 shares in less than a day. I am blown away by the uptake of these templates. Phew! I could've woken up to 100 likes and 13 shares. People have been eagerly waiting for guidance and as soon as they get it, they go for it. I have to avoid getting too many submissions that look the same. I start drafting more templates to ensure we have many unique submissions to the select committee. I make a new template specifically for parents and allies. But at one point, there are so many people on the Google Doc that it breaks up. I keep making new templates, but I quickly lag behind the demand. This is a good problem to have.

Just as I battle it out with the churches, an influential group of TERFs write template letters to encourage people to submit against banning conversion therapy for trans people. They have international connections. They are getting people from the UK to help increase the number of submissions against the ban. There is no way for Parliament to figure out what submissions come from outside New Zealand.

I am not afraid of the TERFs. If they want to go head-to-head with me, I will do it. I make a plea to our neighbouring countries to make submissions to ban conversion therapy. Activists from USA,

Canada, Australia, the Pacific Islands and some parts of Europe appear in droves to make submissions. We turn the Justice Select Committee on its head.

My success at getting the submissions does not impress everyone. Some trans advocates are upset that I am not advocating enough to protect trans people from conversion therapy. They tell me that the movement to ban conversion therapy is so 'unpopular' because it is attached to me. There is a lot of unnecessary competition between trans people. Some think we are playing a zero-sum game. With that logic, if I make it or get applause, then there is no space for anyone else. Some trans people put me down in the pursuit to make it themselves. The movement is not unpopular. It holds the record for most-signed petition. The templates I have written have been opened over half a million times. The thing is, they are upset and that is the end of their action. They do nothing to help.

I am getting criticised by the political left because they disagree with my campaigning strategy. I am being condemned by the churches for advocating against their God-given right to 'cure' queer people. I am being harassed by the right-wing groups. But the worst is being judged by my own community for not fighting hard enough. The queer community is quick to ignore that I am one person trying to carry the weight that should be shared by all. Instead, I carry the weight of their judgement alongside the weight of the fight.

The criticisms don't stop there. The elitist political junkies come out guns blazing. Politicians, academics and political junkies allege me of corrupting the select committee process by making the templates. I am working with thousands of people — queer folk and allies, a community that has an inherent distrust of the state. This is the state that criminalised us. Queer folk are already less likely to engage with the state's processes. The matter is also deeply personal for queer folk. For some it is traumatising to relive their experience of conversion therapy as the debate rages. The templates are a relief for them. Having a template means that they can be a part of the process without putting themselves through the turmoil of investing their scarce energy on defending their humanity.

For many, just the feeling they get by contributing to the process of banning conversion therapy is healing. Folk who have not been traumatised by the state, and have the resources and education to be actively engaged in political processes, do not understand the symbolic importance of just feeling like you are involved. The countless number of people who tell me they would not have made a submission if it weren't for the templates is enough reason to justify the existence of those templates.

There is nothing joyful about constantly putting myself in harm's way to protect my community when that very community turns around and tells me I am not doing enough. It sucks. I am staying up till 3 a.m. every night creating submission templates, and I sit in my room thinking, *Why I am doing this at all? Why is any of this worth it?*

And then I remember the excruciating pain I felt as a kid when no one had my back. The shame I felt when my Class 2 English teacher made me stand through the entire class for nail polish. The loneliness I felt when I had to sit in my room and listen to Guddi, Naffi, Sweta, Dolly, Polly and Bittu play on the road. The endless crying when the elders beat me in the temple. The fear, walking through school alone because no one wanted to be friends with the weird kid. The terror I saw in Zahid's eyes. I must do this even if it destroys me.

The Justice Select Committee closes for submissions on 8 September. I have done everything I can and I pray it is enough.

Despite the churches and the TERFs' efforts against the conversion therapy ban, we outnumber them. There are over 107,000 submissions, and over 80% are in favour.

The CTAG is invited to make an oral submission at 2.30 p.m. on Thursday 16 September to the Justice Select Committee. Harry, Shannon and I make the submission. Alongside the criticisms of the bill, I want the Labour party to know that we are watching them. I submit:

> This is a challenge to the Labour Party. You hold a majority
> at every stage of the process. Whatever Bill we receive
> after the select committee will be what you decide to put
> in front of us. There is nothing the National Party can do to
> stop this ban and they need to accept this. If they choose
> to stay on the wrong side of history, that is on them. But the
> Labour Party needs to stand up to bigotry and fight back.

28
Summer
lovin'

The night sky is reddish-brown. I open the window to let the breeze in and lie on my bed staring out the window. I feel a stinging sensation on my arm and slap myself. The bugs and insects have come in through the window. The stars adorn the sky like diamonds spread on an unending sheet of feathered darkness. The smell of freshly cut grass swirls around me like a tornado. The insect bite is starting to itch.

I adore the calmness about summer. The Justice Select Committee won't report back for a while. Thank heavens. I have not been this still since I turned seventeen. I am at peace. I am ready for summer. I want the sun to roast my body and stew my brain. I have done too much thinking this year.

I download Tinder again and start swiping aimlessly. I do not know what I am looking for, or if someone is looking for someone like me. The responses I have been getting on Tinder are either from people who love me so much they put me on a pedestal and worship me or people who hate my guts. There is no in-between. I have not dated since Frederic passed away. The movement demands all my energy and time, and that is making me very lonely and sad.

One Of Them

I match with Wyatt on Tinder. His eyes sparkle and his face is decorated with the perfect stubble. He messages first. I don't message anyone first on Tinder. Believe it or not, I am shy. I type as quickly as I can to him and catch myself smiling like a fool at the screen. After a few days, Wyatt's Tinder account disappears. Damn.

My head fills up with questions. Did he unmatch me? Did he not like me after talking to me? Did I have a bad sense of humour? No, that can't be it. I am funny. Maybe he did not find me attractive. I close the app and chuck my phone in the pile of blankets on my bed. I am not upset. Dating apps rarely work. I am comfortable with the inactivity. I think I got my hopes up, which was entirely my fault.

To my good fortune, Wyatt already follows me on Instagram. My face lights up like a kid in a candy shop when I see a message with a little image of his face pop to the top of my messages. He has sent a message. I am excited about Wyatt, and although I assumed he did not like me, I open the message with a grin so wide my cheekbones get in the way of my sight. He explains that he lost access to his Tinder and could not reply to me. Oops. I tend to assume the worst. I see he tagged me in a story a while ago. The story has now disappeared, but the notification remains. He says it was a story about conversion therapy.

One morning he messages me to hang out. I am working my hospitality job and do not see his message till the hangout time has passed. We have not spoken to each other in the last few days. I did not want to bother him. My internal dialogue tells me that I will annoy him if I message first. If not that, then I feel like I am coming across as desperate.

I tell him I have been working. He is cool about it, and he asks me out on a date on a different day. I make a nervous but excited squeal sitting at work and look around to see if anyone saw me. It is funny how the butterflies never leave your stomach even after you've done this ritual of waiting before.

Wyatt picks me up from home and drives us to a beach. I am wearing my favourite blue wide-leg trousers and a floral shirt that matches what Wyatt has on. I am horrible at giving instructions. I tell Wyatt that the road is turning. He knows the road is turning. He is driving on it. I miss the exit, but I do not tell him we've missed an exit. I wait for the app to reconfigure itself and continue giving instructions. We go in circles sometimes. I am sure he notices but he does not complain. Wyatt probably thinks I am a fool. I should focus on the map. But I want to look at his face instead. He is gentle on the eyes. We arrive at the beach. We sit ourselves on a large rock just above the water and the sand. The summer light starts its dance on my forehead and moves on to the crystal-blue water. The sea floor has been deposited with sharp corals. I am not going in. The sun is toasting our skin, but the water is still cold.

Wyatt and I have many things in common. We are both studying: me at the University of Auckland and him at Auckland University of Technology. I law and he nursing. We both love to read and want to write one day. We are both ambitious — we have big goals, and we have a plan to achieve them. But I am a cat person, and he is a dog person — how did I look past this incompatibility?

We have a great first date, but I cannot tell if Wyatt likes me or not. We flirt a lot after our first date, so I assume it was a success. He is working night shifts at Middlemore. He sends me random pictures from work. He always has his tongue out in his selfies. He is a golden retriever in human form.

I ask him out on the second date. We meet in Grey Lynn Park. The trees have slept in. The peaceful singing of the birds married with the booming noise of the basketball game and cackling children on the swings and slides is waking the park up. The grass is a little moist.

One Of Them

We sit under the trees people-watching as I listen to him talk about the new books he is reading and his odd but important fascination with diabetes. He tells me he is going to do a fast in the coming days. I am a little concerned. The temperature is rising, and he is living the van life. He drops me off to my voiceover recording at Spark's studio, where I am soon to shoot a commercial. We are becoming close, but I still cannot tell my place with Wyatt. For fleeting moments I feel we drift further apart after each date. I do not want to be overbearing. I give him the power to decide if we are still dating after each date.

After our second date, Wyatt sends me a copy of a book he is reading. We are making a thing out of this, and I adore it. Receiving the book from him is a relief. The same day I receive it, Wyatt messages me to ask if I will go with him outside Auckland for our third date. We are on a roll.

I bounce lightly on my feet, biting my nails and tapping my phone across my hand, thinking about how to respond. I feel a mix of apprehension and excitement. I have not dated for a while. I have never left the city with a guy. I am nervous. But I am serious about Wyatt. I say yes. I have a shoot with *Viva* in the morning and then we leave Auckland for three days.

We stop at Countdown to buy groceries for the time we will be away. As frivolous as it may appear, walking through the supermarket and picking out the right chilli, pineapple, shells and meat for our tacos feels very special. I remember the feeling I got as a kid in Fiji in the supermarket watching the straight couples with their children shopping for their families. I never imagined I would walk through a supermarket with my date. I have to pinch myself.

I can't help but notice people looking at us shopping with disgusted faces. We are revolting to them. I feel the judgement and a little fear, but with Wyatt, I am starting to do things Frederic and I wanted to do but were too afraid to. Wyatt and I are, for a moment, what I really needed to see as a queer kid going grocery shopping with Ma, Pa and Sweta. We are what I always wanted. I do not know the kind of upbringing Wyatt had. I am not sure if his parents were homophobic to him and treated him poorly as a kid. This is not the right time to ask him, but I wonder how he experiences this moment.

Wyatt drives us to our Airbnb. My brain feels like it is a car at a four-way intersection and all the lights are green. Should I go? Should the other cars go? Uh oh, all the cars accelerate at the same time, and we cause an accident. Wyatt has a difficult time making sense of my incoherent rants. He does not complain, but he does point out that I don't make sense sometimes.

As we get closer to our destination, Wyatt mentions that we have not kissed yet. After Frederic's passing, I have avoided dating or being intimate with anyone. No one makes me feel safe like Frederic. My experience with Tyler stays with me. Every time I go to be intimate with men, Tyler is there. I can feel him on top of me, I can feel him groping me, and kissing and biting me. I cannot get him out of my head. If anything gets too close to my face, I freeze. It is harrowing how Tyler gets to move on and I am still trapped in his car.

'Mm-hmm,' I respond to Wyatt, trying to avoid the topic. I don't want to tell Wyatt about Tyler. I tell him that I had a not-so-pleasurable experience with Tyler but that is it. I think it will make me less appealing to him if I tell him what Tyler did to me. I am damaged goods, and I feel inadequate and unattractive every time I think about it. I do not want to ruin our getaway with such a heavy conversation. Wyatt is functioning under the impression that I, like any other twink in their prime, have a high body count, and am excellent at sex. Wyatt has admittedly had sex with at least 40 people before me. I do not even know 40 gay men.

I am nervous that I do not know what I am doing with Wyatt, but I have held back for so long that I don't have any time left to keep avoiding being intimate with people I like. I am afraid life will pass me by. I feel I can trust Wyatt, but that does not make me good at sex immediately. When Wyatt kisses me for the first time, I freeze. He gets my Blistex lip balm all over his lips.

Wyatt is moving to Tauranga next year and I am staying in Auckland. Lying next to him in bed, I ask him what we are. Wyatt says we are dating but he has no plans for us after he moves. It is just settling in that this may be a summer fling. Was I silly to think it was going to be more? He asks if I like girls' clothes or boys' clothes more before telling me that someone like me is new to him. Living as nonbinary is new to me too. I don't have answers to his questions.

Wyatt is the second person I've opened myself to since Tyler. I do not want him to think I am a coward or, worse, that I am not interested in him. I become insecure in my body. I feel ugly. I feel inadequate and lonely after the first night with Wyatt. The next day he tells me that he is afraid I do not know what I am doing. He is referring to my sexual experiences.

I am not mad at Wyatt for my bad experiences and lack of good experiences. He is not at fault. I don't know where to take my resentment. Am I angry at Tyler? Am I angry at society for creating a world that forbids queerness and prevented me from experiencing things non-queer people did years before me? Am I angry at the elders, teachers and church leaders who made me at pain with my queerness?

We have an awkward drive back down to Auckland. Wyatt puts on a political podcast to avoid conversation. I think he is trying to create distraction. We have not ended our dating situation, and we aren't talking about it either. I know we are over. Wyatt says he does not like to label things.

After returning, Wyatt does not speak to me till a day before he is leaving for Tauranga. He insists on taking me for a drive. It is raining heavily. He takes us along Tamaki Drive, but there is nothing to see. Everything is flooded. Wyatt finally speaks. 'So, we were dating, and now we are not.' That was clear to me, so I am in agreement. 'I don't want to be your daddy,' he adds.

Wyatt continues to say I am not at the same level as him, emotionally, spiritually and professionally. I think the truth is I may have ruined his summer break with bad sex before he moved to Tauranga.

Wyatt came into my life during a turbulent time, and he left me when Adele released *30*. I start to hate my body again, feeling inadequate.

I have been a summer fool. Let's cry to 'I Drink Wine'.

29
The Labour party declined

I am not over Wyatt. I do not think I will be for a while, but there is no time for emotions and tears. The Conversion Practices Prohibition Legislation Bill has come back to the House unchanged after the select committee process.

We asked the Justice Select Committee to include people of all ages in the conversion therapy ban. The Labour party declined.

We asked the Justice Select Committee to ensure redress to victims. The Labour party declined.

We asked the Justice Select Committee to remove the requirement for the Attorney-General to consent to prosecution. The Labour party declined.

We asked the Justice Select Committee to include intersex people in the conversion therapy ban. The Labour party declined.

The Labour party declined all the amendments CTAG, and I, asked for. We broke the record for the number of select committee submissions, and still the Labour party managed to ignore everything we asked for. It is too late now for any changes. The Labour party has a majority, and they are going to pass the bill they want. No one can stop them.

I want to ensure that people know that the Labour party has

ignored the voices of grassroots activists. As soon as I see the Bill, I launch a petition titled 'Actually Ban Conversion Therapy'. I ask the Labour party to amend the Bill through Supplementary Order Papers at the Committee of the Whole House. The petition gains over 19,000 signatures in two days.

On 8 February, the Conversion Practices Prohibition Legislation is read for a second time. The Parliament gallery is closed to all members of the public due to Covid-19. I could not be in attendance for the first reading of the Bill. I cannot attend the second reading either. I am sitting in my room and watching the debates on Parliament TV. The Bill is going to pass its second reading, but I am not convinced that this bill is good enough. The Labour party will not accept any of my recommended changes at the Committee of the Whole House either.

The speeches begin and Simon O'Connor on behalf of the transphobes in the National party gets up to say:

> I've got lesbian and gay friends who are concerned
> about this bill because actually that community, the
> LGBTQIA+ community, is not a single cohesive unit. As one
> acquaintance put to me, 'As a gay man,' he said, 'actually, in
> today's day and age I'd be afraid that I'd be told actually I'm
> really just needing something gender affirming — I'm not
> actually a gay man; I'm a woman and I just need to explore
> that.' He feels his identity as a gay man could be erased
> with the modern zeitgeist at the moment that is more
> around transgender issues. That's his experience.

Oh, it is uncomfortable to watch. If his speech is a plane, he isn't landing it; he is crashing. Simon says he talked to a gay man who told him that banning conversion therapy would mean that gay men would be erased and forced to live as trans women. Absolute junk. No one is trying to make cisgender gay men trans. Not a single person.

In fact, the opposite happens all the time. Trans people are bullied and shamed into detransitioning. Marja tweets that Simon's speech is 'cringeworthy', which in all honesty is a generous assessment. It is embarrassing that this is the quality of legislators we have in New Zealands Parliament.

The speeches come to an end rather quickly, and the Speaker of the House, Trevor Mallard, asks the House to vote. The House votes through voice. Those in favour say 'Aye' and those against say 'No'. The loudest wins. Trevor says the voices sound like 120 to none. The ayes have it.

Chris Penk calls for a personal. Trevor allows it, and the votes are taken again. 113 ayes and 7 noes. Labour, Greens, Māori party and ACT vote in favour. The National party vote is split. The seven against are from National MPs: Simon Bridges, Simeon Brown, Melissa Lee, Simon O'Connor, Shane Reti, Louise Upston and Michael Woodhouse.

30
Mourning the movement

'Shaneel!' Pa screams. My parents have never yelled out for me so desperately. I am studying from home and don't want to be disturbed. I sluggishly put decent clothes on. I open my bedroom door only to drown in black smoke; under our terrace is a sea of flames. Our apartment is on fire.

I freeze. The fire is not so scary, but the smog devours the path. It is hard to see or breathe. It starts to smell of charred wood. The fire is raging, and I have to get out of here.

But everything I own, my laptop, my clothes, my bed, my shoes, I mean everything, is in the house. My life flashes before my eyes. Everything we own will be set ablaze. I grab my phone, my laptop, my bank cards — Pa yells at me to call the fire brigade.

I snap back to reality. If I do not get help quickly, everything will be gone for sure. I have an adrenaline spike. I cannot remember what number to dial. My hands are sweaty, and I can't control my fingers. I keep typing extra numbers and deleting them. I finally call 111 and ask for the firefighters. While they make their way to our building, I try to get everyone out. Pa yanks the water blaster attached to the side of our eight-apartment complex and puts the fire out before the firefighters can arrive.

We are lucky. We do not know what started the fire. It started in the apartment under ours, but terror strikes me to the core. Did someone try to burn down my place? My address has been leaked and I have received threats to my door before. It is plausible that a crazy right-winger might have tried to act on their threats to kill me.

The Committee of the Whole House is scheduled for tonight. I cannot watch it. We have the power off. I leave home and go to dinner with my friends Logan, Jessee and Cinnamon. Meanwhile, the Minister of Justice considers and declines all the requests in my petition at the Committee of the Whole House.

I am in summer school doing a paper called 'Animals and the Law'. My exam is on 15 February. The third reading for the Conversion Practices Prohibition Legislation Bill is on the same night. This is what everything has been building up to for the last five years. This is the worst possible alignment. How can I focus on my exam when the work of my life is coming to fruition on the same night? I sit my exam and finish it as quickly as I can.

As soon as I close my laptop, I realise this is the last time this bill will be read. I put on a red suit and a sparkly black metal crop top and make my way to my friend Josh McCormack's apartment. We take an Uber to Countdown to buy as many snacks as we can in ten minutes. Josh and I run across Countdown throwing things in a basket. We are running late. The third reading of the Bill will start in a few minutes, and I am not going to miss this. We check out and take another Uber to Max's place.

We know the Bill is going to pass. We have known this at every stage of the process, but that still does not help the nerves, the excitement, the euphoria. We spend the night clapping, yasssing and yelling at the TV.

The National MPs who are voting against banning conversion therapy do not show up for the speeches. Labour MP Kieran

McAnulty takes the National party's speaking time and swings 'em by the weave. Kieran says, 'It wasn't my intention to speak on this, this evening, but there have been more opportunities than we expected — because we thought that there would be some members tonight that would wish to speak in opposition to this bill. Given that there were seven members that voted no, we thought that some of them would come to this House tonight and explain to the New Zealand people why.'

Just before 9 p.m., the Conversion Practices Prohibition Legislation Bill passes. 112 votes in favour and 8 votes against. National MPs Simon Bridges, Simeon Brown, Melissa Lee, Todd McClay, Simon O'Connor, Chris Penk, Shane Reti and Michael Woodhouse vote against banning conversion therapy. I send a cheeky tweet to Labour MPs Ayesha Verrall and Tamati Coffey, asking them to tell Trevor Mallard to blast 'Raining Men' at 9 p.m. as the Bill passes. Trevor does not play it. That remains my personal grievance with him.

We have done it. A movement of five years is over in a few moments. I don't know how to grasp what we have just achieved. My back slumps, and I fall back in my chair, my eyes looking heavenward. I let out a huge breath. A massive weight is lifted off my shoulders. Chini would have lived a different life if conversion therapy was not allowed. I would have grown up like every other child — carefree, enjoying the beautiful things in life, like the parrots singing during the flowering season of *jamun*, lying under the shade of mandarin trees in sizzling hot summers, running barefoot in the streets playing '*Gilli Danda*' and dancing to my favourite Bollywood songs if the elders weren't allowed to abuse me. I would have grown up free from the trauma that haunts me every day if the teachers weren't allowed to beat me. Conversion therapy stole my childhood.

I never knew what was coming next, so I stayed frozen in a constant state of fear. The smallest things startled me. When I hear the words that the ban has passed, my passion softens into a vulnerable cry. A flint of healing sparks within me. I escaped my conversion therapy when I moved to Aotearoa, but I was in survival mode long after I did not have to be. The trauma my body absorbed from the beatings, prayers, insults and fear may never leave me. The moment we ban conversion therapy, the hurt child in me can rest. The panic may finally come to an end. No queer child will be born in an Aotearoa that accepts or tolerates the erasure of their identity. This kind of protection would have changed my life. It would have saved Isireli. It would have protected Zahid.

I spend the rest of the night speaking to media. I have an early start tomorrow morning for more interviews. I go to bed after 1 a.m., and I am up at 6 a.m. There is another note on my door saying 'Hang yourself'. I feel nothing. I pick the note up and burn it and call for celebration of our victory. I refuse to live in fear. Last night humanity won. Queer rights are human rights. The ban on conversion therapy was not only a win for queer people, it was also a win for humanity. When the church leader approached me at Middlemore Hospital's reception, I told myself that 'I can, I must and I will ban conversion therapy'. Last night, I did.

The *New Zealand Herald* publishes an article on 16 February 2022 headlined '"Enjoy the victory": Activist calls for celebration despite death threats after conversion therapy ban.' Bob McCoskrie, the director of Family First, a group that venomously opposed the conversion therapy ban, complains that the article 'made groups and individuals who opposed the Bill look very bad and willing to physically threaten people.' The *New Zealand Herald* article did not mention Bob or Family First. The Media Council does not accept Bob's case. The Council rules that 'the story has not been shown to be inaccurate. There is nothing to indicate that Lal did not receive the note or that Lal's word on this is in question.' I wonder why Bob felt he looked bad because I told the media I received a death threat.

I wake up to a lot of messages. I am tagged under a picture by many people. I open the post and — Holy shit! *Vogue* has posted about me and the movement to ban conversion therapy. I never imagined as a little brown queer kid that I would make it out of my little village. I believed that my life would begin and end with hiding. But here I am, in *Vogue*, showing people that life changes. Mine changed.

I am at an all-time high, but the next few weeks aren't so kind. I wake up feeling miserable every day for the next month. I am coming off a victory feeling tired and empty. I wanted to be perfect. I handled the movement flawlessly and forged an image of having it all together, but I have been making it all up as I go along. The movement took my last few years of being a teenager. Perhaps I am resentful that I had to make those sacrifices when my non-queer friends did not.

The 2022 summer pumps lava through my body. I feel tired after sleeping for ten hours. I have an uncontrollable urge to cry. I am not upset or sad. I feel loss. I lost the movement that for years I cared and worked for, and I lost the purpose and drive it imbued me with. I wanted to ban conversion therapy, and I wanted to do it as quickly as possible. So why am I mourning the movement after the ban has passed?

The last few years have been incredibly exhausting, but I kept myself together because I was working towards a goal. If I stopped, the movement would stop with me. I convinced myself I needed to keep working or I would be failing my community. It was crushing. Now that it is over, the responsibility has lifted, and I have to sit in silence with my feelings. It is a terrifying experience. All the emotions I have suppressed for the last five years rush at me at once. I drown in them.

I do not have a sense of self, independent of the movement. It only takes people a few days before they start asking me what I am going to do next. I don't know what I want to do. I just know I want to be free.

I don't want to be tolerated, protected or accepted. Tolerated for what? There is nothing in my life that requires people to tolerate me. Protected from whom? Protection is only extended to me if I abide by the rules of patriarchy. My mission is to make patriarchy fear me. And acceptance? I am who I am. That is not for anyone else to accept. I do not give anyone power over me to accept me. I want to be free.

Being involved in politics changed how people see me. They see me as angry. I am forced to maintain a professional public persona to be taken seriously, especially with my identity. If I did not have to do politics, I probably would not. It is stressful. I would rather do skincare and look like a glazed doughnut, binge-watch *Survivor* and *Dancing with the Stars*, sip peppermint tea and roll around with kittens. The notions of innocence and vulnerability are not afforded to me because I am brown, immigrant, poor and queer. I need to be miserable to be supported and exceptional to be celebrated.

The beautiful thing about being so young is that I have time. I have the time to show people who I really am. I do not understand why I am rushing, and who I am running this race against. I have been silly trying to do so much in so little time when I have the rest of my life ahead of me. I have time to find myself. I will find myself. I am a masterpiece and a work in progress. I will love myself endlessly while I continue to grow.

Oh, I have so much growing to do. But I also have so much I want for me. I want to tell my parents who I am, and I hope they will learn to love me. I do not have a coming-out story. The priests chained and dragged me out of my closet. Ma and Pa know who I am. My life is broadcast on the news every week. I am no longer trying to change the channel when I know I am going to be on the news. I no longer hide the *New Zealand Herald* when I am in it. They deserve to get to know me. Trauma isn't built only by the things you experience. It can form because of the things you do not experience. My queerness built a wall between Pa and me. I do not know him.

I do not have a perfect ending. I am nowhere near the end. Twenty-two is hardly a start. But as I grow older, I want to go back to being a playful, carefree young person. I wish that I was not afraid of showing the world all parts of me. I want to live a free life.

I know I have some youth left but I am terrified I have allowed life to pass me by. I have missed out on all of the core experiences that people my age were experiencing. I regret it. I made the same mistakes as all people my age, but mine were broadcast for fifty thousand people to see. There were consequences for me in situations that warranted no consequences, and harsher consequences for me in situations that did. The fear limited my growth. It stopped me from learning because I was never allowed to not know better. It made me afraid of being who I really am. It made me afraid of taking risks. It made me afraid of living life. I wish myself a safe return to me.

Acknowledgements

My story began in a little village in Fiji, and while things did not go how I needed them to, I have very special memories of my village. I am fond of the days I spent sewing doll clothes with Guddi and Naffi and running on the road barefoot playing *tin paani* with Bittu, Polly and Dolly.

I am nostalgic for the days I spent with Nani. It was brave of Nani to go against everyone and let me play with her sarees. An act so little allowed me to express what I was feeling.

I am grateful for the people who made me feel like I belonged in the times I felt the most unsafe and unwelcome.

Moving to Aotearoa saved my life. To the pastor who offered me conversion therapy while I was volunteering at Middlemore Hospital: you reignited the fire in me.

To Jenny Salesa, who chose me as her youth MP in 2018: you changed my life. I wouldn't be where I am today if I did not get the chance to speak at Youth Parliament. At nineteen, when speaking at Youth Parliament, I did not appreciate what I had signed up for. The next few years turned out to be the most phenomenal yet traumatic years of my life.

In the movement to ban conversion therapy, I met incredible people. I will always be thankful to Marja Lubeck, who showed unwavering allyship to the queer community. I honour the co-activists and survivors I fought alongside to ban conversion therapy. To those who trusted me with leading the movement: you may not realise it, but you gave me a chance to heal myself.

I am indebted to Théo (and Zahid) for teaching me I am worthy of love. In a world full of hatred for queer people, finding my people was hard, but when I did find them, I learnt there was nothing I wouldn't do for them. To Wyatt: thank you for reminding me of the importance of loving myself.

I am thankful to my friend Sabby Jey and Jessie Gurunathan who with an email helped me sign with my management, WeAreTenzing. I acknowledge Amanda Cox and Dan Sing, who got me a meeting with Allen & Unwin within a month of my joining WeAreTenzing. I thank my publisher Michelle Hurley for believing in my story and Fleur Beale and my editor Madison Hamill for helping me tell my story.

My life has been a rollercoaster. I sometimes threw my hands in the air to enjoy the highs. There were moments I held on tight out of fear of falling off. And often, I felt like jumping out of the ride. I am grateful for the people who stuck around as I grew from an impulsive, hurt and sometimes confused teenager into an intelligent, kind, passionate and happy adult.

For those who hated on me as I evolved: thank you for giving me a backbone made of titanium.

I thought my life would start and end with hiding. Life changes because sometimes the stars align. I am grateful for how my life played out, the good and the bad. If they hadn't, I wouldn't be writing this acknowledgement.

To my sister Sweta, thank you for coming around to understand I am who I have always been. To Ma and Pa: I hope one day you see your child is no different from the one you loved as Chini.